The Battle of Waterloo

Books in the Battles Series:

The Battle of Belleau Wood
The Battle of Britain
The Battle of Gettysburg
The Battle of Hastings
The Battle of Marathon

The Battle of Midway
The Battle of Waterloo
The Battle of Zama
The Inchon Invasion
The Invasion of Normandy

✤ Battles of the Nineteenth Century ✦

The Battle of Waterloo

by David Pietrusza

Lucent Books, P.O. Box 289011, San Diego, CA 92198-9011

Library of Congress Cataloging-in-Publication Data

Pietrusza, David, 1949-
    The Battle of Waterloo / by David Pietrusza.
        p. cm. — (Battles of the nineteenth century)
    Includes bibliographical references and index.
    Summary: A detailed account of the events leading up to a
celebrated battle of the nineteenth century, the battle itself, and
results of Napoleon's military failure.
    ISBN 1-56006-423-4 (alk. paper)
    1. Waterloo, Battle of, 1815—Juvenile literature. 2. Napoleon I,
Emperor of the French, 1769–1821—Military leadership—Juvenile
literature. 3. Napoleonic Wars, 1800–1815—Campaigns—Belgium—
Waterloo—Juvenile literature. [1. Waterloo, Battle of, 1815.
2. Napoleonic Wars, 1800–1815—Campaigns. 3. Napoleon I, Emperor of
the French, 1769–1821.] I. Title. II. Series.
DC242.P53 1996
940.2'7—dc20   95-31686
                                                            CIP
                                                            AC

Contents

Foreword

Almost everyone would agree with William Tecumseh Sherman that war "is all hell." Yet the history of war, and battles in particular, is so fraught with the full spectrum of human emotion and action that it becomes a microcosm of the human experience. Soldiers' lives are condensed and crystallized in a single battle. As Francis Miller explains in his *Photographic History of the Civil War* when describing the war wounded, "It is sudden, the transition from marching bravely at morning on two sound legs, grasping your rifle in two sturdy arms, to lying at nightfall under a tree with a member forever gone."

Decisions made on the battlefield can mean the lives of thousands. A general's pique or indigestion can result in the difference between life and death. Some historians speculate, for example, that Napoleon's fateful defeat at Waterloo was due to the beginnings of stomach cancer. His stomach pain may have been the reason that the normally decisive general was sluggish and reluctant to move his troops. And what kept George McClellan from winning battles during the Civil War? Some scholars and contemporaries believe that it was simple cowardice and fear. Others argue that he felt a gut-wrenching unwillingness to engage in the war of attrition that was characteristic of that particular conflict.

Battle decisions can be magnificently brilliant and horribly costly. At the Battle of Thaspus in 47 B.C., for example, Julius Caesar, facing a numerically superior army, shrewdly ordered his troops onto a narrow strip of land bordering the sea. Just as he expected, his enemy thought he had accidentally trapped himself and divided their forces to surround his troops. By dividing their army, his enemy had given Caesar the strategic edge he needed to defeat them. Other battle orders result in disaster, as in the case of the Battle at Balaklava during the Crimean War in 1854. A British general gave the order to attack a force of withdrawing enemy Russians. But confusion in relaying the order resulted in the 670 men of the Light Brigade's charging in the wrong direction into certain death by heavy enemy cannon fire. Battles are the stuff of history on the grandest scale—their outcomes often determine whether nations are enslaved or liberated.

Moments in battles illustrate the best and worst of human character. In the feeling of terror and the us-versus-them attitude that accompanies war, the enemy can be dehumanized and treated with a contempt that is considered repellent in times of peace. At Wounded Knee, the distrust and anticipation of violence that grew between the Native Americans and American soldiers led to the senseless killing of ninety men, women, and children. And who can forget My Lai, where the deaths of old men, women, and children at the hands of American soldiers shocked an America already disillusioned with the Vietnam War. The murder of six million Jews will remain burned into the human conscience forever as the measure of man's inhumanity to man. These horrors cannot be forgotten. And yet, under the terrible conditions of battle, one can find acts of bravery, kindness, and altruism. During the Battle of Midway, the members of Torpedo Squadron 8, flying in hopelessly antiquated planes and without the benefit of air protection from fighters, tried bravely to fulfill their mission—to destroy the *Kido Butai,* the Japanese Carrier Striking Force. Without air support, the squadron was immediately set upon by Japanese fighters. Nevertheless, each bomber tried valiantly to hit his target. Each failed. Every man but one died in the effort. But by keeping the Japanese fighters busy, the squadron bought time and delayed further Japanese fighter attacks. In the aftermath of the Battle of Isandhlwana in South Africa in 1879, a force of thousands of Zulu warriors trapped a contingent of British troops in a small trading post. After repeated bloody attacks in which many died on both sides, the Zulus, their final victory certain, granted the remaining British their lives as a gesture of respect for their bravery. During World War I, American troops were so touched by the fate of French war orphans that they took up a collection to help them. During the Civil War, soldiers of the North and South would briefly forget that they were enemies and share smokes and coffee across battle lines during the endless nights. These acts seem all the more dramatic, more uplifting, because they indicate that people can continue to behave with humanity when faced with inhumanity.

Lucent Books' Battles Series highlights the vast range of the human character revealed in the ordeal of war. Dramatic narrative describes in exciting and accurate detail the commanders, soldiers, weapons, strategies, and maneuvers involved in each battle. Each volume includes a comprehensive historical context, explaining what brought the parties to war, the events leading to the battle, what factors made the battle important, and the effects it had on the larger war and later events.

The Battles Series also includes a chronology of important dates that gives students an overview, at a glance, of each battle. Sidebars create a broader context by adding enlightening details on leaders, institutions, customs, warships, weapons, and armor mentioned in the narration. Every volume contains numerous maps that allow readers to better visualize troop movements and strategies. In addition, numerous primary and secondary source quotations drawn from both past historical witnesses and modern historians are included. These quotations demonstrate to readers how and where historians derive information about past events. Finally, the volumes in the Battles Series provide a launching point for further reading and research. Each book contains a bibliography designed for student research, as well as a second bibliography that includes the works the author consulted while compiling the book.

Above all, the Battles Series helps illustrate the words of Herodotus, the fifth-century B.C. Greek historian now known as the "father of history." In the opening lines of his great chronicle of the Greek and Persian Wars, the world's first battle book, he set for himself this goal: "To preserve the memory of the past by putting on record the astonishing achievements both of our own and of other peoples; and more particularly, to show how they came into conflict."

Chronology of Events

1789
French Revolution starts on July 14 when Parisian mob storms the Bastille, a national prison.

1791
Royal family attempts to flee France and is captured at Varennes in northeastern France.

1793
Louis XVI and Marie-Antoinette are guillotined; Napoléon Bonaparte defeats the British at Toulon.

1794
Napoléon is named commander of artillery for the Army of Italy; Robespierre is overthrown; Napoléon is arrested for conspiracy and treason.

1795
Napoléon crushes a royalist insurrection at Tuileries Palace.

1796
Napoléon is named commander of the Army of Italy; Napoléon marries Joséphine de Beauharnais.

1798
Napoléon invades Egypt.

1799
After successful coup d'état Napoléon is named one of three consuls governing France.

1800
Plebiscite legitimizes Napoléon's dictatorship.

1801
The Peace of Lunéville ends hostilities between Austria and France and expands France's borders.

1802
The Peace of Amiens ends hostilities between Great Britain and France; Napoléon is named consul for life.

1804
The Code Napoléon is first issued; Ney and Soult are made marshals; Napoléon crowns himself emperor of France.

1805
Admiral Nelson destroys the French fleet at Cape Trafalgar; Napoléon defeats Austrians and Russians at Battle of Austerlitz.

1806
Joseph Bonaparte is appointed king of Naples; Louis Bonaparte is appointed king of Holland; Napoléon imposes the Decree of Berlin; Napoléon defeats the Prussians at the Battle of Jena and Auerstedt.

1807
Napoléon defeats the Russians at the Battle of Friedland; Jérôme Bonaparte is appointed king of Westphalia; Napoléon imposes the Decree of Milan; Russia surrenders with the Treaty of Tilsit; Napoléon seizes Portugal.

1808
Joseph Bonaparte is made king of Spain; Napoléon personally leads armies in Spain.

1809
Napoléon defeats Austrians at Wagram.

1810
Napoléon marries Maria Luisa, daughter of the emperor of Austria.

1811
Birth of a son, François-Charles-Joseph, to Napoléon.

1812
Wellington defeats the French in Spain; Napoléon begins invasion of Russia; Napoléon engages the Russians at the Battle of Borodino; Napoléon captures Moscow.

1813
Wellington defeats the French at the Battle of Vitoria; Napoléon is defeated at the Battle of Nations.

1814
Paris falls to the Allies; Napoléon abdicates and is sent in exile to Elba; Congress of Vienna convenes.

1815
February 26   Napoléon escapes from Elba.

March 1   Napoléon lands at the Golf Juan-les-Pins.

March 7   Napoléon reaches Grenoble.

March 20   Napoléon occupies Paris.

May 2   Murat defeated at the Battle of Tolentino.

June 12   Napoléon leaves Paris to lead attack against Wellington and Blücher.

June 14   Napoléon reaches the Franco-Belgian border.

June 15
3:00 a.m.   French troops cross the Belgian border.

5:00 a.m.   General Bourmont deserts to the Prussians; General Vandamme finally receives word he is to lead the advance, against the Allies.

Noon   Napoléon reaches Charleroi.

3:30 p.m.   Ney and Vandamme reach Charleroi; Wellington receives word of Napoléon's advance into Belgium.

4:00 p.m.   Blücher arrives at Sombreffe.

6:00 p.m.   Prussians retreat from Gilly.

5:00–7:00 p.m.   Wellington orders his commanders to concentrate near Mons and Ath.

7:00 p.m.   Ney turns back to Gosselies.

June 16
3:00 a.m.   Wellington hears of Napoléon's advance; marches on Quatre Bras.

10:00 a.m.   Wellington reaches Quatre Bras.

11:00 a.m.   Napoléon reaches the front lines; learns that Blücher has moved forward; Ney issues his first marching orders of the day.

1:00 p.m.   Wellington meets Blücher near Brye.

2:00 p.m. Reille's French Second Corps assembles at Quatre Bras; Napoléon sends Ney a message to attack Wellington at Quatre Bras; Wellington leaves Brye for Quatre Bras.

2:30 p.m. Napoléon attacks at Ligny.

3:15 p.m. Napoléon sends a second message to Ney to attack Wellington at Quatre Bras.

4:00 p.m. Ney receives Napoléon's first message to attack Wellington and intensifies his attacks.

6:00 p.m. Allies receive additional reinforcements at Quatre Bras; Drouet retreats from Ligny and starts for Quatre Bras; last Prussian troops committed at Ligny.

6:30 p.m. Wellington launches successful counterattack.

7:30 p.m. Napoléon orders the Imperial Guard to storm Blücher's center; Blücher retreats toward Wavre.

9:00 p.m. Battle of Quatre Bras ends with Allies regaining all lost ground; Prussians evacuate Ligny; Drouet finally arrives at Quatre Bras.

11:00 p.m. Napoléon returns to Fleurus.

June 17
4:00 a.m. Pajol sends an inaccurate report to Napoléon of a disorganized Prussian retreat toward Namur.

6:00 a.m. Napoléon receives Pajol's report.

7:00 a.m. Napoléon receives word from Ney that Wellington is still at Quatre Bras.

7:30 a.m. Wellington learns of Blücher's defeat at Ligny and orders a retreat to begin at 10:00 a.m.

8:00 a.m. Napoléon orders Ney to take up positions at Quatre Bras.

9:00 a.m. Wellington receives word that Blücher is retreating toward Wavre; responds that he is taking up defensive positions to the south of Waterloo; Ney receives Napoléon's 8:00 a.m. orders but does nothing to prevent Wellington's retreat.

11:00 a.m. Napoléon begins march to Quatre Bras.

2:00 p.m.. Napoléon reaches Quatre Bras but finds no fighting; pursues Wellington himself.

June 18
2:00 a.m. Wellington learns from Blücher that Bülow, Pirch, and Zieten will meet him that day.

3:00 a.m. Napoléon awakes.

4:00 a.m. Bülow begins march toward Waterloo.

8:00 a.m. Grouchy sets out for Wavre.

9:00–11:00 a.m. Bülow reaches Saint Lambert.

11:00 a.m. Napoléon orders a frontal assault on Wellington.

11:35 a.m. Battle of Waterloo begins with French attack on Hougoumont; Grouchy is unaware of significance of distant cannon fire and refuses to join Napoléon.

Noon Remainder of Blücher's forces reach Saint Lambert.

1:00 p.m. Napoléon learns Bülow is on his northeast flank and sends a message to Grouchy to attack Bülow.

1:20 p.m. French artillery near la Belle-Alliance opens fire; Ney and Drouet begin main French assault.

3:30 p.m. Napoléon orders Ney to take la Haye Sainte.

4:00 p.m. Prussian forces arrive to aid Wellington; Ney's cavalry unsuccessfully attacks the Allied center.

4:30 p.m. Bülow attacks the French flank.

5:00 p.m. Grouchy, at Wavre, receives Napoléon's 1:00 p.m. message; Bülow takes Plancenoit.

6:00 p.m. La Haye Sainte falls to the French.

7:00 p.m. Plancenoit recaptured by the French; French Old Guard attacks Wellington's center.

8:00 p.m. The Old Guard is defeated; Napoléon, defeated, retreats.

8:15 p.m. Wellington orders a general advance; rout of French begins.

9:00 p.m. Allies retake Plancenoit.

June 19
1:00 a.m. In retreat Napoléon arrives at Quatre Bras.

6:00 a.m. Napoléon arrives at Charleroi.

10:00 a.m. Thielmann abandons Wavre to Grouchy.

10:30 a.m. Grouchy learns of Napoléon's defeat and abandons Wavre.

June
Congress of Vienna ends.

June 22 Napoléon abdicates a second time.

June 28 Louis XVIII is restored to the throne.

July 3
Napoléon reaches Rochefort; French government signs an armistice with the Allies.

July 15 Great Britain formally accepts Napoléon's surrender.

August 5
Ney is arrested in Paris.

October 13
Murat is executed in Italy.

October 15 Napoléon arrives in exile at Saint Helena.

November 20
Treaty of Paris formally ends the war.

December 7
Ney is executed in Paris.

1821
May 5 Napoléon dies at Saint Helena.

1840
December 14 Napoléon is reburied in Paris.

A Clash of Giants

The Battle of Waterloo was justifiably the most celebrated battle of the nineteenth century, and it remains one of the most famous and significant battles of all time. It was a clash of military giants that ended the career of its most brilliant participant. It contained the classic elements of bravery, suspense about its outcome and, yes, colossal blunders.

Unlike few other events in history, *Waterloo*, as a word, has become a part of the language, meaning a dramatic, disastrous, and final end to a career. The original case was that of French emperor Napoléon Bonaparte.

Napoléon rose to prominence as emperor of France, only to lose it all at the Battle of Waterloo.

Napoléon, originally a humble artillery officer, emerged from the turmoil of the French Revolution to seize power over the French nation and eventually over most of Europe. When the French Revolution began, France fought other European nations for survival. Napoléon, not satisfied with survival, wanted glory. France became an empire, and Napoléon became its emperor. His family became the ruling family of several vassal states, totally subservient to France.

But French rule created growing resentment among other European peoples, and that helped create new feelings of nationalism. From Spain to Prussia to Russia the Continent's peoples rose up against the French.

In 1812 Russia's czar, Alexander I, refused to help Napoléon in economic warfare against

Great Britain, France's most tenacious enemy. A frustrated Napoléon then assembled his huge Great Army to conquer Russia. That force reached Moscow but was soon destroyed by a combination of the harsh Russian winter and skillful Russian strategy. Only a handful from Napoléon's battered army returned from this disastrous campaign.

Napoléon's enemies now closed in on him, and in 1814 he was forced to abdicate, or step down, as emperor. The victorious Allies exiled him to the small Mediterranean island of Elba and restored the former Bourbon ruling house to the throne of France. But by early 1815 Napoléon had escaped from Elba, landed in France, and reclaimed power.

Napoléon's former enemies, Great Britain, Prussia, Russia, and Austria, vowed to destroy him again and assembled huge armies at France's northern frontier, or border, for that purpose. Napoléon knew he had to strike first and destroy his opponents before they could join together and destroy him.

This was his strategy as he invaded Belgium in June 1815. There an Anglo-Dutch force under the British duke of Wellington and a Prussian force under General Gebhard von Blücher had gathered. Napoléon would strike one and then the other, hoping to smash any desire the Allies had for further warfare.

At the Battle of Ligny Napoléon defeated Blücher, but Napoléon's subordinate, Marshal Michel Ney, missed an opportunity to defeat Wellington at the Battle of Quatre Bras. Napoléon then made mistakes of his own, failing to follow up on his besting of Blücher and being slow to attack Wellington. When he finally did, Blücher's forces had recovered from their defeat and joined with Wellington in battling Napoléon.

The Battle of Waterloo, fought on June 18, 1815, saw Napoléon's army on the attack for most of the day. Toward evening the French were on the verge of overrunning Wellington's troops. But Wellington never wavered, and his troops wore out the attacking French. As the evening approached, the last French charge failed. The Anglo-Dutch force counterattacked, and with the Prussians now pummeling the French right flank, Napoléon's army absolutely collapsed in one of the great routs of military history.

Why did Napoléon lose at Waterloo? The easy answer is that he was simply outnumbered by his opponents, the British, Dutch, and Prussians. That was true enough, but it was not the real answer.

Napoléon had once conquered all of Europe. His brilliant military strategies had led to great triumphs at such battles as Marengo and Jena and Austerlitz. But that genius was long gone, expiring somewhere in his ill-fated Russian campaign. Once he had been able to almost instantly analyze a situation and to act forcefully and correctly on it. Now he procrastinated, entrusting

The Battle of Waterloo signaled the end of the French Revolution.

his armies to inferior generals, such as Ney and Marshal Emmanuel de Grouchy, and badly underestimating his opponents' steadfastness.

Many also blame Napoléon's health for his loss. At Waterloo he suffered from a variety of ailments, including stomach pains, hemorrhoids, and a wracking cough. His behavior seemed sluggish. He was slow to issue orders and slow to respond to messages, and he preferred receiving the cheers of his adoring troops rather than working out the plans for what needed to be done.

As Napoléon misplayed his hand, his main adversaries, Wellington and Blücher did not. Wellington had successfully battled against Napoléon's armies in Spain and Portugal and was a master of defensive tactics. At Waterloo he would be fighting from a strong defensive position. Blücher had long hated Napoléon. His determination would not only help keep his army together after its defeat at Ligny, but would also keep it moving relentlessly toward a linkup with Wellington.

After Waterloo Napoléon abdicated once more. This time he was exiled to the isolated south Atlantic island of Saint Helena, from which there would be no escape. As Napoléon spent his last years on this remote speck of land, the crowned heads of Europe attempted to restore the old order. At first they succeeded, but they could not hold back the rising tides of nationalism and reform that the French Revolution had unleashed on Europe. Eventually the more destructive forms of Europe's nationalism would help lead to two world wars.

The defeated Napoléon, however, would not be forgotten. A Napoleonic cult soon developed. The military glory of his empire continued to dazzle many, with thousands of books written about him and hundreds of thousands of people in France and even throughout Europe still remembering him fondly. A second Napoleonic empire, headed by his nephew, would even rule France from 1852 through 1871. Like the first empire, it too ended in military disaster.

At Waterloo the era of the French Revolution and of Napoléon came formally to an end, but the days of complex alliances and massive armies engaged in deadly warfare across the map of Europe, of deadly nationalistic rivalries, and of egoistic dictators was only just beginning.

CHAPTER ONE

The Rise of Napoléon and the Napoleonic Wars

Louis XVI is threatened by the mob in front of the palace at Tuileries. Louis would be swept off the throne and guillotined during the French Revolution.

Napoléon Bonaparte was a man of his times. As such, two distinct eras in French history, the Enlightenment and the French Revolution, shaped his personality and career. Without these events Napoléon would most likely have remained an obscure artillery officer in the French army.

Enlightenment ideas, including what were considered to be scientific beliefs in the power of reason, the natural goodness of humanity, and the inevitability of progress, had helped give birth to the French Revolution. Both movements attempted to free people from the bonds of the old order, whether it was established religion or the tyranny of royalty and nobility. The unexpected result of these movements, however, would result not in a republic but in an emperor, Napoléon I.

In 1789, when Napoléon was twenty years old, the French Revolution erupted. Ultimately the Bourbon monarchy of Louis XVI and his queen, Marie-Antoinette, would be swept away in a bloodbath of ever increasing radicalism and suspicion. The remaining European monarchs feared that the spread of revolutionary ideals might sweep them off their own thrones. They reacted by waging war on France. By 1792 Austria, Sardinia, and Prussia were at war with France. A year later Great Britain, Spain, and the Low Countries also would be fighting the new republic. France needed highly skilled military leaders to equal the odds.

Revolution

Napoléon soon earned fame as a commander of artillery. In December 1793 he defeated the British at Toulon, and at just twenty-four he was promoted to the rank of brigadier general and given command of France's forces on the Italian peninsula, the Army of Italy.

Napoléon's career in this period, however, was more political than military. In July 1794 the revolutionary leader Maximilien Robespierre fell from power and along with many of his followers was executed. Napoléon, considered one of Robespierre's disciples, was stripped of his command and arrested for treason. The charges were dropped, but he was not restored to his former command. Instead, he was offered control of French artillery in western France.

Sulkily he refused that post and remained in Paris. At the time those who supported the Bourbons' return—monarchists, or royalists—were gathering strength. In Paris in October 1795 they attempted a coup d'état, or military overthrow of the government. Napoléon was second in command of artillery and was given the key responsibility of defending the revolutionary government at the Tuileries Palace. He ruthlessly turned his guns on the plotters and saved the new republic from the monarchists. But he ominously informed his superiors "I warn you, once my sword is out of the scabbard I shall not replace it until I have established order."

Napoléon during his days as a lieutenant of artillery. Always ambitious, Napoléon's daring—and the fact that many officers had been guillotined or had fled into exile during the French Revolution—allowed him to rise quickly through the military ranks.

The Political General

Many of the old-line French military officers had been aristocrats and unsympathetic to the revolution. The new regime swept them away, creating an opportunity for soldiers like Napoléon to rise rapidly through the ranks. The ambitious Napoléon became increasingly influential in French politics, either protecting or destroying French governments through the use of his troops.

Whereas in October 1795 the twenty-six-year-old artillery officer had rescued the government from its monarchist and more moderate enemies on the right, in February 1796 he clamped down on its even more radical opposition. As a reward he again received command of the Army of Italy. The Napoleonic legend was about to begin.

His army was hardly fit for battle, but Napoléon urged his soldiers on to victory against his Austrian enemies. In one proclamation

When Napoléon arrived at his new command in Italy, his troops were demoralized, starving, and ill equipped. His personal charisma and strategic genius quickly turned them into a victorious fighting unit.

he relied less on revolutionary fervor for inspiration than on dreams of greatness: "Soldiers, you are naked, badly fed. . . . Rich provinces and great towns will be in your power, and in them you will find honor, glory, wealth. Soldiers of Italy, will you be not wanting in courage and steadfastness?"

Napoléon's army marched from victory to victory, decisively defeating the Italian states of Sardinia, Parma, Modena, the Papal States, and finally Austria. Napoléon was not satisfied with military successes, however. That September, on Napoléon's orders, General Pierre Augereau launched a successful coup d'état, or coup, against the current French government, or Directory, which consolidated Napoléon's influence in Paris.

France remained at war with Great Britain. The French government wanted Napoléon to invade Great Britain, but Napoléon thought a seacoast invasion too risky. Instead he advanced an even more ambitious and chancy scheme: an invasion of Egypt.

The heart of Great Britain's overseas empire was India. Napoléon thought that if he could seize Egypt, then under the nominal rule of the Ottoman Turks, he could block British trade with India, bring Great Britain's economy to its knees, and force that nation to conclude a peace with him. In 1798 Napoléon reached Egypt and defeated all opposition. However, in a decisive battle fought by the French and British navies, the British admiral Horatio Nelson destroyed the French fleet in what became known as the Battle of the Nile. Napoléon was now

Napoléon greets the Great Sphinx while in Egypt. Ever fascinated by Egypt, Napoléon later sent a research expedition to document the wonders of the pyramids.

trapped in Egypt. He responded by marching through Palestine into Syria. At Acre he was defeated, and he retreated to Egypt.

Napoléon's disastrous adventures in the Middle East encouraged France's enemies on the European Continent. Austria and Russia joined Great Britain and Turkey in opposing France, and France suffered great reverses in Italy. At home royalist agitation increased. Napoléon, the republic, and France itself seemed in jeopardy.

In August 1799 Napoléon, having learned of French military reverses and the weakness of the Directory, abandoned his Egyptian army, which remained stranded there until a truce enabled it to leave in 1801. This action failed to discredit him in French eyes. "His disappearance into the Orient," noted historian Ida Tarbell, "had all the mystery and fascination of an Eastern tale. His sudden reappearance had something of the heroic about it. He came [back to France] like a god from Olympus, unheralded, but at a critical moment."

Napoléon had returned to France resolved to lead a coup to seize control of the government, crush the monarchists, and save the nation from foreign invasion. By the time he returned, however, the situation had changed dramatically; French armies were victorious in the field, and the Bourbon sympathizers were waning in popularity. There was simply no need for a Napoleonic coup.

What had not changed was Napoléon's ambitions. So, during the night of November 9–10, 1799, Napoléon and two others, supported by much of the military stationed in Paris, seized power. Napoléon was named first consul. Previously, three consuls had shared executive power in France, but now the other two took orders from Napoléon. "The whole machinery of the government," wrote Ida Tarbell, "was now centered in one man."

First Consul

Napoléon's regime as France's first consul was unusually energetic, both at home and in the field of battle against France's foreign enemies.

The French chose in a national plebiscite, or general vote, in February 1800 to approve a new constitution legitimizing Napoléon's dictatorship. He now had the authority to appoint most of the French government—ministers, generals, magistrates, and bureaucrats. He even had great power in naming members of the legislature. Napoléon set about reorganizing the entire structure of the French government. He created the Bank of France and strengthened the police, higher education, and judiciary. To bolster his support on the left, he legitimized the distribution of land among the peasantry and passed laws restricting the freedoms of returned émigrés, those nobles who had fled from France in the wake of the revolution. To win support on the right, he made

Napoléon, along with two others, (Cambacêrês and Lebrun) is installed as first consul at the Luxembourg Palace.

peace with the Roman Catholic Church, signing a concordat, or agreement, with Pope Pius VII that recognized the secular, or non-religious, nature of the French state but that gave French Roman Catholics greater freedom of religion.

Napoléon's greatest domestic achievement was his Code Napoléon. Issued in March 1804, it organized France's hodge-podge of existing legislation from the 366 separate local codes that had previously existed. The Code Napoléon consolidated the gains of France's middle class, abolished the privileges of the old nobility once and for all, and established religious tolerance. To this day it serves as a basis for the French legal system.

Amazingly while all of this was occurring domestically, France was at war with a wide-ranging alliance of monarchies that were trying to undo the work of the French Revolution. Napoléon returned to Italy in 1800 and decisively defeated the Austrians, who had been besieging the French at Genoa in northern Italy, at the Battle of Marengo. The Peace of Lunéville in February 1801 restored the original frontiers of Gaul, France's ancient ancestor, extending French borders to the Alps in Italy and to the Rhine River in Germany. Great Britain remained at war with France, but Napoléon forced the defeated nations of Russia, Sweden, Prussia, and Denmark to form the League of Armed Neutrality against the British, designed to isolate it diplomatically and in terms of trade. In March 1802 the Peace of Amiens concluded hostilities between France and Great Britain.

Peace only increased Napoléon's hunger for titles and power. In August 1802 a rigged plebiscite, which suspiciously passed by a margin of 3.5 million votes to 10,000, made Napoléon consul for life and gave him the right to name his own successor. The French Revolution, which had begun by toppling one monarch, was on the verge of creating a new one.

Napoléon crosses the Alps at Saint Bernard to extend France's borders into Italy.

War Again

Although now at peace with Great Britain, Napoléon once again sought to weaken that nation through economic sanctions. That is, he forced other European nations to enact high tariff barriers, or import taxes, against British goods. And he added new territory to his domain, annexing the Piedmont region on France's southeast border and in 1800 acquiring the vast Louisiana Territory in North America from Spain. Great Britain and France continued to distrust each other. In 1803 they argued over ownership of the tiny but strategic Mediterranean island of Malta. With that as the excuse, in May 1803 Great Britain again declared war on Napoléon.

To defeat Great Britain, which was fighting France without the aid of Austria, Russia, Prussia, or any Continental ally, Napoléon planned to invade. To do so, he gained the support of Spain. As a prelude to invasion, the combined Spanish and French fleets would draw the British fleet into battle and gain control of the seas. At Cape Trafalgar on the southwest coast of Spain, in October 1805 Britain's Admiral Nelson again destroyed Napoléon's plans for glory. Although Nelson died of wounds suffered in the battle, the Franco-Spanish armada, or fleet, was destroyed. Never again would Napoléon seriously contemplate invading his persistent British opponent.

Admiral Nelson during the Battle of Trafalgar, which would lead to the defeat of the Spanish Armada.

The House of Bonaparte

In May 1804 Napoléon became the monarch of France in name as well as in fact. Yet another plebiscite made him emperor of the French and created a Bonaparte dynasty. As other emperors had done before him, Napoléon summoned the pope to Paris to crown him in December 1804. At the last second, however, Napoléon grabbed the crown from Pius VII's hands and in a monumental act of egoism crowned himself. To solidify his power, Napoléon began naming his relatives to rule as kings of other European nations: his brother Joseph as king of Naples and later of Spain; his brother Jérôme as king of Westphalia, in Germany; his brother Louis as king of Holland; his brother-in-law Marshal Jean-Baptiste Bernadotte as king of Sweden; his brother-in-law General Joachim Murat as king of Naples after Joseph became king of Spain; his sister Marie-Anna Élise as princess of Lucca and Piombino in central Italy; and his stepson Eugène de Beauharnais as viceroy of the kingdom of Italy.

To further consolidate his claims to royal privileges, in 1809 Napoléon divorced his first wife, Joséphine de Beauharnais, who had not borne him an heir, and in 1810 married Archduchess Maria Luisa, daughter of Francis I, emperor of Austria. She bore him a son, François-Charles-Joseph, in March 1811.

(Above) Despite divorcing Joséphine because she could not produce an heir, Napoléon remained in love with her, visiting her and asking for her advice throughout his life. (Right) To consolidate his power, Napoléon offered key positions to his relatives, including Jérôme, who became king of Westphalia, Germany.

Many considered that when Napoléon became emperor, he betrayed his youthful ideals and those of the French Revolution. Late in his life he defended his actions. "I closed the gulf of anarchy and cleared the chaos," he told the Count de las Cases, "I purified the Revolution, dignified Nations and established Kings. I excited [provoked] every kind of emulation [imitation], rewarded every kind of merit, and extended the limits of glory! This is at least something!"

But war continued with Great Britain, and as time passed, the British enlisted Russia, Austria, Naples, and Sweden to fight against Napoléon. Napoléon defeated Austria at Ulm in October 1805 and two months later at Austerlitz. Austria and Naples surrendered, and Joseph Bonaparte received the crown of Naples in 1806.

Austria's reverses did not keep Prussia from entering the struggle against Napoléon, but in October 1806 its armies met a decisive defeat at Jena and Auerstedt in eastern Germany. Napoléon's successes continued in 1807 as he defeated the Russians at Friedland in East Prussia. That June Napoléon and the Russian czar Alexander I met at the East Prussian town of Tilsit and made not only peace, but an alliance. France would control western Europe; Russia would rule eastern Europe.

Still Great Britain remained opposed to Napoléon. France again resorted to economic warfare. The Decrees of Berlin in 1806 and Milan in 1807 imposed a ban, known as the Continental System, on trade with Great Britain. But not everyone wished to do without British goods, particularly Portugal, a longtime British ally. To bring Portugal into line, Napoléon conquered that nation in 1807. That invasion not only failed to close Portugal's ports to Great Britain, it also caused a series of massive problems for Napoléon. To subdue Portugal, French troops had to cross Spain, a loyal ally of Napoléon. At first this presented no problem, but French troops soon turned to occupying Spain as well as Portugal.

Napoléon placed his brother Joseph on the throne of Spain. Fiercely independent, the Spanish struggled against French rule for years.

The Spanish people openly revolted, and Spain's Bourbon monarch abdicated. Napoléon replaced him with his brother Joseph, the former king of Naples. "From beginning to end the transfer of the Spanish crown from Bourbon to Bonaparte was dishonorable and unjustifiable," observed Ida Tarbell. "This was not a conquest of war, not confiscation on account of the perfidy [treachery] of an ally, not an attempt to answer the prayers of a people for a more liberal government." It was aggression, pure and simple.

The people of Spain now fought on with even greater cause for resentment, conducting guerrilla, or unconventional, warfare and inflicting large casualties on the French army. The Spanish were aided by a British general Napoléon would later face directly at Waterloo, Arthur Wellesley, better known to history as the duke of Wellington.

Slaughter in Spain

The beginning of the end for Napoléon may first be traced to his adventures on the Iberian Peninsula. When the Spanish people tired of the French presence in their land, they began a war of national liberation that relied less on regular armies than on guerrilla tactics.

Where previously French armies had fought against armies that were supporting ancient dynasties, in this case they fought an army of people who were battling for their homeland. The result was a war of incredible bloodshed and brutality.

The Spaniards resorted to sabotage, attacking French convoys and mounting surprise attacks on French garrisons. Aiding the Spaniards to ultimately free themselves was an English army under the command of Arthur Wellesley, later made the duke of Wellington. Wellington also employed irregular and brutal tactics, resorting to a scorched-earth policy of destroying everything he could not hold. Even Napoléon's personal presence in Spain could not bring final triumph for the French armies. He referred to the country as "my Spanish ulcer." By the summer of 1813, after sustaining 300,000 casualties, France was driven out of the Iberian Peninsula.

Recording the images of this terrible war was the famed Spanish artist Francisco José de Goya y Lucientes. Goya's series of etchings *Disasters of the War*, painted between 1810 and 1814, graphically chronicled French atrocities and are an eternal testament to the horrors of warfare. Ironically, although Goya recorded French war crimes, during the occupation he served as court painter for Joseph Bonaparte. When the French were finally ousted from Madrid, Goya had to hide for three months from Spaniards who considered him a traitor.

A copy of Goya's paintings that made up his Disasters of the War. *In it, a French soldier smugly eyes his Spanish victims.*

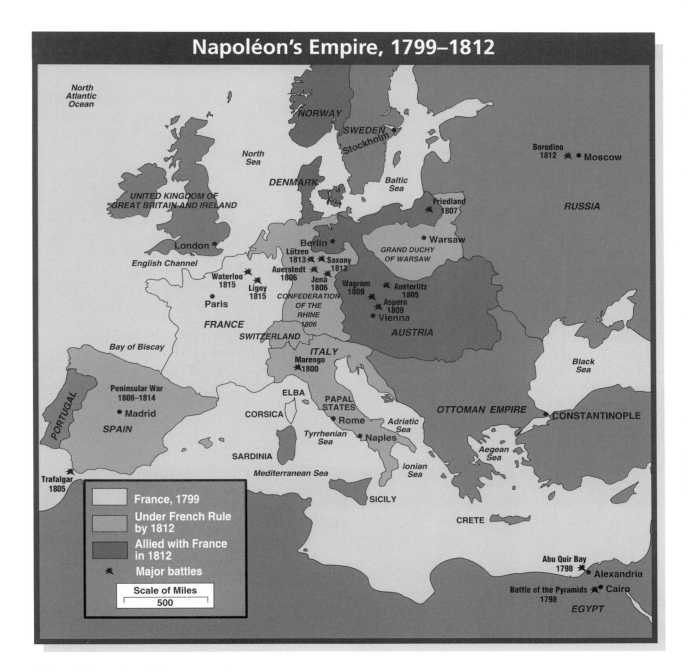

Napoléon's Empire, 1799–1812

North Atlantic Ocean

NORWAY

SWEDEN
Stockholm

North Sea

DENMARK

Baltic Sea

Borodino 1812 ✳ • Moscow

RUSSIA

UNITED KINGDOM OF GREAT BRITAIN AND IRELAND

Friedland 1807

London

English Channel

Berlin

Lützen 1813 ✳ ✳ Saxony 1813

Auerstedt 1806

Jena 1806

Waterloo 1815

Ligny 1815

Paris

FRANCE

CONFEDERATION OF THE RHINE 1806

Warsaw

GRAND DUCHY OF WARSAW

Wagram 1809

✳ Austerlitz 1805

Aspern 1809

Vienna

AUSTRIA

SWITZERLAND

Bay of Biscay

ITALY

Marengo 1800

ELBA

PAPAL STATES

CORSICA

Rome

Adriatic Sea

Tyrrhenian Sea

Naples

Black Sea

OTTOMAN EMPIRE

CONSTANTINOPLE

Aegean Sea

Peninsular War 1808–1814

Madrid

SPAIN

PORTUGAL

SARDINIA

Mediterranean Sea

Ionian Sea

Trafalgar 1805

SICILY

CRETE

France, 1799

Under French Rule by 1812

Allied with France in 1812

✳ **Major battles**

Scale of Miles
500

Abu Quir Bay 1798 ✳ • Alexandria

Battle of the Pyramids 1798 ✳ • Cairo

EGYPT

The Empire Unravels

Despite severe difficulties in Spain and Portugal, Napoléon seemed at the peak of his power. Most of Europe was under his control. Many of his relatives sat on the thrones of a series of French vassal states. Yet because of his desire for total control of the Continent, it all quickly unraveled.

First, Austria rebelled against his rule and again took up arms. Napoléon recalled some of his troops from Spain and quickly defeated the Austrians at Wagram, near Vienna, in July

Disaster in Russia

Starting in 1806 Russia's Alexander I and France's Napoléon had been allies, but the relationship was soon strained. First, Alexander refused to allow the imperial upstart Napoléon to marry his sister. Second, Alexander opposed Napoléon's idea of re-creating a Polish state largely from Russian territory. Lastly, Alexander refused to comply with Napoléon's trade blockade against Great Britain.

In retaliation Napoléon assembled an army of over 450,000 men and in June 1812 advanced rapidly into Russia. The Russians failed to stop him at the bloody Battle of Borodino, and on September 14 the French army entered Moscow. The Russians then showed how truly serious they were in opposing Napoléon's schemes by burning 80 percent of Moscow to the ground.

For five weeks an indecisive Napoléon camped in what was left of the city, waiting for Alexander to beg for peace. While Napoléon waited, his supplies grew scarce, and the onset of the fierce Russian winter drew near.

Finally he resolved to retreat south to Smolensk through Kaluga, but Russian forces blocked his way. The French moved west on another route, and as they did, their discipline evaporated. As in Egypt, Napoléon abandoned his troops, hurrying back to Paris to organize new regiments. The French retreat was barely better than a rout. Napoléon's reluctant Prussian and Austrian allies abandoned him. He lost all his artillery and 200,000 horses. Only 40,000 soldiers survived the ill-fated invasion.

Said Alexander I: "The fire of Moscow lit up my soul, I then got to know God and became another man." Alexander was not the only person energized by Moscow; soon all of Europe would turn on Napoléon.

1809. Next, Russia's Alexander I continued to resist participating in Napoléon's Continental System of economic warfare against Great Britain. In the spring of 1812 Napoléon gathered his Grande Armée (Great Army) of 435,000 in Poland. He hoped this show of force would convince the czar to bow to his will and enact high tariffs against British goods. But Alexander would not bend, and in June 1812 Napoléon invaded Russia. It was perhaps the greatest strategic mistake of his long career.

Throughout the summer and fall of 1812, Napoléon easily advanced into Russian territory. Alexander's commander, Prince Mikhail Kutuzov, retreated steadily, refusing to engage Napoléon's Grande Armée. As Kutuzov withdrew, he pursued a scorched-earth policy, destroying all he left behind, so that Napoléon would have nothing to aid his invasion. With French supply lines stretched hundreds of miles and the fierce Russian winter approaching, this proved a wise strategy.

Kutuzov and Napoléon did fight at Borodino, seventy miles southwest of Moscow, on September 7, but that battle's bloody result was inconclusive. The French continued marching forward and entered Moscow on September 14. That day the Russians set most of Moscow afire. As in Egypt, Napoléon had attained his goal, but in the process he was trapped far from home by his enemies.

Napoléon began the long retreat back to the Russo-Polish border. By November his Grande Armée was in tatters. Because of Russian opposition and the harsh weather, fewer than forty thousand soldiers remained in his main force, and of those, only ten thousand were in sufficiently good shape for combat. Napoléon's Russian campaign was one of the greatest military disasters in history.

News of Napoléon's rout spread like wildfire among his enemies—both in France and without. In Paris that October General Claude-François de Malet attempted an unsuccessful coup against Napoléon. Former foreign minister Charles-Maurice de Talleyrand-Périgord and former police minister Joseph Fouché plotted against him as well. Both Prussia and Austria withdrew their troops from contact with the Grande Armée. In Italy nationalist feelings grew.

Hungry and ill clothed for the fierce Russian winter, Napoléon's troops retreat from Moscow toward the Russo-Polish border.

Napoléon, however, regrouped and prepared to fight again. At first it appeared he might stave off disaster. He defeated the Prussians and Russians at the Battles of Lützen and Bautzen in eastern Germany, but his rebuilt army was on the verge of exhaustion. Austria nearly rescued him, proposing an international conference at Prague. The peace terms would have left Napoléon emperor, slightly reduced France's boundaries, and abolished such French vassal states as the Grand Duchy of Warsaw and the Confederation of the Rhine.

The once decisive Napoléon could not make up his mind, and Austria withdrew its offer. It was an irreversible mistake on his part. His army in Spain was defeated at Vitoria in June 1813. At Leipzig in eastern Germany that October, in the Battle of Nations, his Grande Armée was demolished. In Belgium, Holland, and Germany, his old allies turned against him. In Italy even his brother-in-law, Joachim Murat, changed sides.

Louis XVIII became king of France in 1813.

In November 1813 the Allies—Austria, Prussia, Russia, Holland, and Great Britain—again offered Napoléon a peace settlement. Again he refused. Now they closed in on France itself. Even there Napoléon faced growing opposition and discontent. By late March the Allies had reached Paris, and Talleyrand invited the brother of the deceased Louis XVI, guillotined in 1793, to assume the throne as Louis XVIII.

Marshal of France Michel Ney led Napoléon's marshals in informing the emperor that the game was up, that he would have to abdicate. He did so on April 6, 1814.

It appeared—incorrectly—that the Napoleonic adventure was at an end.

CHAPTER TWO

Exile and Return

On April 6, 1814, Napoléon abdicated as emperor of the French, naming his three-year-old son his successor. Not surprisingly, the victorious Allies wanted nothing to do with Napoléon's choice. Napoléon II and his mother, Maria Luisa, returned to her family's home in Vienna. Napoléon II would never rule France, nor would he ever see his father again.

The Bourbon Restoration

But if a Bonaparte would not rule France, who would? Under pressure from the British, the Allies restored Louis XVIII to the nation's throne. It was a mistake. Turning the calendar back to 1789 would have been difficult under any circumstances. Under the unimpressive Louis XVIII it was nearly impossible.

Louis XVIII had not learned much from the events of the last two decades. He believed in absolute monarchy and the divine right of kings, even though few of his subjects still did. Beyond that he was an incredible glutton, stuffing himself full of enormous amounts of food. His girth made him nearly immobile. The rich foods he ate gave him gout and further incapacitated him.

Louis XVIII not only ate, he spent. Before long he had frittered away much of the fortune Napoléon had acquired from the spoils of war. Such lavishness incensed his subjects, who suffered from growing unemployment as France converted from a wartime to a peacetime economy. French men and women also chafed under the burden of military defeat. Not long before, they had ruled Europe. Now the victorious Allies who occupied France carted away large quantities of French military equipment such as cannons and munitions.

A Dispirited Emperor

Napoléon took defeat badly. The Allies could have executed him, and many wanted to. Instead they allowed him to retain his title of emperor and to rule over the tiny Mediterranean island of Elba, in the Piombino Strait, seven miles southwest of the Italian mainland. He could take one thousand soldiers with him, and the new French government agreed to support Napoléon with a handsome annual pension of two and a half million francs plus an additional yearly sum of two million francs for his attendants.

On April 14, 1814, Napoléon left his residence at Fontainebleau in a coach bound for the port city of Fréjus, where he would board a ship for Elba. Four commissioners, representing Austria, Prussia, Great Britain, and Russia, accompanied him. It was not an easy journey. Napoléon's enemies incited mobs to jeer at him along the way, and he feared for his life. At one point he even adopted a disguise to help ensure his safety. Hiding in such fashion was an act the usually brave but now desperate and despondent Napoléon regretted for the rest of his life.

At the Palace of Fontainebleau, Napoléon (center, left) extends his hand to the commander of his treasured Old Guard before entering his traveling carriage bound for exile on the island of Elba.

To the roar of a 101-gun salute, Napoléon landed on Elba on May 4, 1814. At Elba's capital of Portoferraio almost the entire island of 13,700 souls turned out to greet him. Napoléon informed Elba's governor, Brigadier General Jean-Baptiste Dalesme:

Napoléon leaves from Saint Raphaël for the island of Elba, where he is greeted by a 101-gun salute.

> General, I have sacrificed my rights in the interests of the nation, while reserving for myself the sovereignty and property of the Island of Elba, which has been consented to by all the Powers. Be so good as to have this new state of affairs made known to the inhabitants, and the choice I have made of their island—because of its climate and the gentleness of their ways—for my sojourn [temporary stay]. Tell them they will be the constant object of my sincerest interests.

Île du Repos

No one will ever know what really went on in Napoléon's mind as he settled in to exile on Elba, but initially he seemed resigned to his tiny domain.

He referred to it as the *île du repos,* "isle of repose," and busily set about improving his new realm: He created new roads, a quarantine station, a theater, fortifications, new vineyards and farms, and a reorganization of Elba's tariff and tax structure. It was the most activity the backward little island had seen in centuries.

To the island's British commissioner, Sir Neil Campbell, Napoléon jauntily wrote in September 1814: "Henceforth I want to live the life of an ordinary justice of the peace. . . . The Emperor is dead and I am no longer of importance to anyone. . . . My only concern is for my little island; I require nothing more of the world . . . than my family, my little house, my cows and my mules."

But certain imperial tendencies never went away. One of Napoléon's first moves was to annex a nearby uninhabited island, which he planned to occupy with thirty of his troops.

"Europe is going to accuse me of already having started on the road to conquest," he joked to Campbell.

Trouble in Paradise

Napoléon's ambitions would have made a prolonged stay on Elba nearly impossible for him, but several other factors aggravated his situation.

The first was highly personal. Napoléon had repeatedly begged his wife, the empress Maria Luisa, to join him in exile with their son. The Allies had not forbidden such a family reunion, but Maria Luisa had no interest at all in joining her husband, and she remained in Vienna, much to the pleasure and relief of her father, Emperor Francis I. Napoléon bitterly informed Campbell, "My wife no longer writes to me. My son has been taken from me just as the children of the conquered were in former times, with which to proclaim and crown their victory."

Another factor was financial. Louis XVIII's foreign minister Charles-Maurice de Talleyrand-Périgord, known as Talleyrand, had seized Napoléon's personal fortune of ten million francs, and the king failed to provide Napoléon with his promised annual allowance. Without that subsidy there was no way Napoléon could maintain his lavish imperial court on Elba.

A third factor was political. The situation in France was changing rapidly. Louis XVIII's already minimal popularity was falling rapidly. Many in Paris sported the violet, the symbol of support for the fallen emperor.

Napoléon's attitude changed. He realized that without French subsidies even this little world that was left him might collapse in a matter of months. Making matters even worse were rumors of Allied plans to exile him to Trinidad or Australia or of plots to kidnap or even kill him. Napoléon's return to France was not only a question of recaptured glory, it was also a matter of personal survival.

He turned suddenly hostile to Sir Neil Campbell, who begged his superiors to come through on their financial promises to Napoléon. "I persist in my opinion," he wrote, "that if Napoléon receives the rent stipulated by the treaties, he will remain perfectly content, barring an extraordinary event in Italy or France."

The Elban Invasion of France

When Napoléon first planned leaving Elba and recovering power in France is not known, but it is believed he made no preparations for escape before February 1815. It was on February 10 that Neil Campbell presented Napoléon with the opportunity for flight. On that date Campbell left Elba for a twelve-day holiday in Florence, Italy. Napoléon instantly sprang into action, securing supplies for a voyage and organizing a small fleet, which consisted of his sixteen-gun flagship, the *Inconstant*, a one-gun sloop, the *Caroline*, one large open boat, and two *feculias*—small sailing vessels—the *Mouche* and the *Étoile*.

This minuscule flotilla was not enough to transport Napoléon's 1,250 men, so he seized a 196-ton private commercial ship, the *Saint-Esprit*. Just after midnight on February 26, 1815, Napoléon set sail to oust Louis XVIII from power and to reconquer France.

(Left) According to legend, in his early days Napoléon was an indefatigable and brilliant battle strategist. (Below) Aboard the ship Inconstant, *Napoléon leaves Elba to reclaim the French throne.*

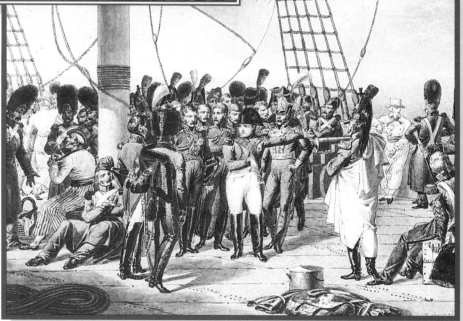

Napoléon realized he could not regain power by force of arms. If his return to France caused a civil war, he could not win it because the Allies would intervene on Louis's side and crush Napoléon. Said the former emperor of France, with tongue firmly in cheek: "I am the sovereign of the Island of Elba and have come with six hundred men to attack the King of France and his six hundred thousand soldiers. I shall conquer this kingdom. Are such things not permitted among sovereigns?"

No, the use of force of arms was not Napoléon's strategy. He had to seize France by force of will.

To that end he appealed to the loyalty of his former soldiers. One poster placed along Napoléon's route proclaimed:

> Soldiers, Come and place yourselves under the flags of your leader; his life is composed only of yours; his rights are only those of the people and yours; his interest, his honor, his glory, are no other than your interest, your honor and your glory. Victory will advance at your charge; the eagle, with the national colors, will fly from steeple to steeple all the way to the towers of Nôtre Dame [cathedral, in Paris]. Then you will be able to show your scars with honor, then you will be able to boast of what you have done; you will be the liberators of your motherland.

Napoléon's small fleet approached land between Cannes and Antibes at the Golf Juan-les-Pins on the morning of March 1, 1815. He was able to escape capture by British ships in part because Campbell had thought he would attempt to land in Italy rather than in France. It was not until 1:00 P.M. that the actual landings took place. Their only opposition came from a local customs official, who demanded that certain health regulations

Napoléon and his troops arrive at Golf Juan-les-Pins on March 1, 1815.

be complied with. When the official's troops, however, saw that it was Napoléon Bonaparte himself who was landing, they exclaimed "C'est Napoléon! C'est Napoléon!" ("It is Napoléon!") and welcomed him wildly. Any thoughts of health regulations were quickly forgotten.

Napoléon's plan—as much as there was of one—was to advance on Paris through the lower Alps, for a more direct route would prove less hospitable. Like lightning word of his landing spread throughout Europe. In 1815 France employed a relatively advanced means of communication, the aerial telegraph. This telegraph was nothing like Samuel F. B. Morse's later invention. It consisted of men atop high observation towers conveying messages by flashing semaphore signals with flags. In this fashion messages could travel as fast as five hundred miles an hour. This particular news may have traveled even faster.

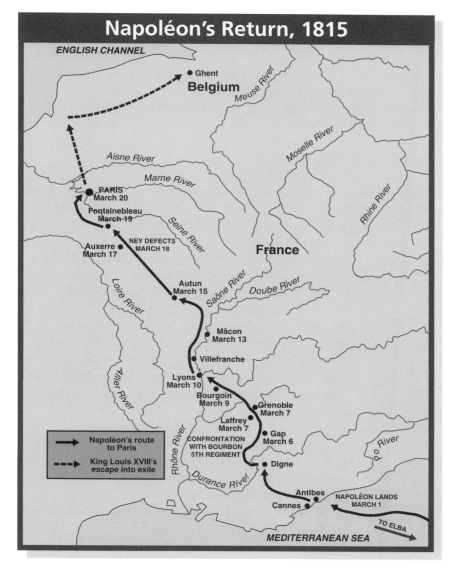

Napoléon's Return, 1815

ENGLISH CHANNEL

Ghent
Belgium

Meuse River

Moselle River

Aisne River

Marne River

Rhine River

PARIS
March 20

Fontainebleau
March 19

Seine River

NEY DEFECTS
MARCH 18

Auxerre
March 17

France

Autun
March 15

Saône River

Doube River

Mâcon
March 13

Loire River

Villefranche

Allier River

Lyons
March 10

Bourgoin
March 9

Grenoble
March 7

Laffrey
March 7

Gap
March 6

Po River

CONFRONTATION
WITH BOURBON
5TH REGIMENT

Rhône River

Digne

Durance River

→ Napoléon's route to Paris

--→ King Louis XVIII's escape into exile

Antibes

Cannes

NAPOLÉON LANDS
MARCH 1

TO ELBA →

MEDITERRANEAN SEA

It reached Vienna on March 7. Since September 1814 the Allied powers had been meeting at the Congress of Vienna, attempting to restore the politics of Europe along prerevolutionary lines. That Napoléon had escaped from Elba while they were still meeting was not in his favor. With all the Allies together in one place, they could easily meet and devise a strategy to crush him once more. Czar Alexander I turned to the hero of the Iberian wars, the duke of Wellington, and remarked, "It is for you to save the world again."

On March 13, 1815, the Congress of Vienna declared Napoléon an international outlaw: "Napoléon Buonaparte [Bonaparte], by again appearing in France with projects of confusion and disorder, has placed himself beyond the protection of the law and rendered himself subject to public vengeance."

Austria, Prussia, and Russia agreed to provide an army of 700,000 under the command of Austria's Prince Karl Philipp zu Schwarzenberg to crush Napoléon. Great Britain promised five million pounds to help finance the army. The duke of Wellington would assume command of an Anglo-Dutch force forming in Belgium, then a part of the Netherlands. Prussia's Field Marshal Gebhard von Blücher would join him, and together they projected a force of 150,000 men to oppose Napoléon on France's northern border.

"I Was a Prince"

Gathering support daily, Napoléon is enthusiastically greeted by the citizens of Grenoble.

The first Bourbon troops to defect to Napoléon were those of the Eighty-Seventh Regiment, stationed in Antibes. Napoléon's small column of troops marched north through the snow-clad Alps, through Digne and Gap.

By March 7 Napoléon had reached Laffrey, just south of Grenoble. There he found his path blocked by the Bourbon Fifth Regiment. Napoléon still knew that if actual fighting broke out, he was finished. He strode toward the royalist troops, who stood there with muskets and bayonets at the ready. Staring at them, he flung on his long, gray overcoat and dared them "to fire upon your Emperor." They threw down their weapons and rushed to join Napoléon's army.

The dash to join Napoléon was now overwhelming. The people of Grenoble welcomed him as a conquering hero. "Before Grenoble I was only an adventurer," Napoléon later boasted; "after Grenoble, I was a Prince."

In Paris many members of the government had felt that Napoléon could easily be crushed. Marshal Ney called his old commander "a mad dog upon

The Congress of Vienna

In 1814 Napoléon was defeated and in exile in Elba, but it also appeared to some observers that the effects of the French Revolution could finally be extinguished. To restore Europe to its prerevolutionary past, the crowned heads of Europe met at the Congress of Vienna.

Austria, Prussia, Russia, and Great Britain took the lead in this congress, but Spain, Portugal, Sweden, and many minor states also attended. Because of the presence of so many dignitaries in Vienna, the assemblage was often as much a social one as a diplomatic one.

Dominating the business of the day were Alexander I of Russia, foreign minister Lord Castlereagh of Great Britain, Count Metternich of Austria, and the able and wily Talleyrand of the defeated French nation.

The first task before the congress was to redraw the entire map of Europe. The Napoleonic wars had changed many of the Continent's old borders, particularly in Italy and in Germany, where Napoléon had reduced the number of political entities from over three hundred to just thirty-nine. The most sensitive problem involved that of Poland. Alexander I, who would rule Poland, wanted Poland's boundaries to be enlarged at the expense of Prussia and Austria. To compensate Prussia, Alexander proposed that the kingdom of Saxony, Napoléon's loyal vassal, be given to Prussia. Finally a compromise was reached in which Austria and Prussia retained portions of Poland, but Prussia received 40 percent of Saxony.

A key principle of the congress was legitimacy, that is, preserving or restoring the reign of the old royal families of Europe. In this manner not only were the Bourbons restored to the throne of France, but also that of Naples. Legitimacy also helped preserve the rule of the king of Saxony.

One issue of no consequence to the men of Vienna was nationalism. Italy and Germany remained disunited. Austria and Russia continued to rule over such nationalities as the Poles, Italians, Hungarians, and Czechs; the Dutch, over the Belgians; and the Danes, over the Norwegians.

Decades later the issue of nationalism would again redraw Europe's boundaries and help lead to two world wars.

---

whom one must fling oneself in order to avoid his savage bite." He bragged, "If I have the good fortune to arrest him, I hope to bring him back to Paris alive in an iron cage!"

Marshal Nicholas-Jean de Dieu Soult, Louis XVIII's minister of war echoed Ney: "Bonaparte thinks so poorly of us that he believes we can abandon a sovereign, legitimate and well loved, in order to share the fate of a man who is no more than an adventurer. He believes it, the madman! And the latest act of lunacy shows it completely."

For all Louis XVIII's faults, however, he realized his own limitations. From the beginning of Napoléon's escape that Louis knew the former emperor would succeed in reclaiming power.

Regiment after regiment flocked to the Napoleonic tricolor, that is, the blue, white, and red flag adopted by the republic in

1789. He advanced to Lyons on March 10, to Mâcon on March 13 and to Auton on March 15. One humorist told of Napoléon's cheekily writing to Louis XVIII: "My Good Brother, there is no need to send more troops; I already have enough."

Ney, who had taken command of a force of thirty thousand to stop Napoléon, began wavering, particularly when he thought of an Allied invasion: "If foreigners set foot on French soil, all France will be for Napoléon! There's nothing left for the King, for his part, but to place himself at the head of his troops, to have himself borne on a litter, so as to fire [inspire] the soldiers and resolve them to fight!"

Napoléon was soon courting Ney. He sent him one message, reading, "I shall receive you as after the battle of Moskowa [Moscow]," a reminder of Ney's bravery in the ill-fated Russian campaign.

On March 18 Ney switched sides, although his embrace of Napoléon was guarded. He warned Napoléon: "From now on the Emperor must govern with one object only, the happiness of the French people and the undoing of the evil which his ambition has brought upon the country." Ney then told his troops: "Officers, non-commissioned officers and men, the Bourbon cause is lost forever!" Louis XVIII now had no doubt at all that he was finished.

On the night of March 19 Napoléon reached his former palace at Fontainebleau, where he had abdicated less than a year before. In the middle of the night Louis XVIII, suffering from gout, entered his coach and quietly fled from Paris, declaring that he wished "to gather strength and seek in another part of the realm, not subjects more loving than our good Parisians, but Frenchmen more advantageously placed to declare themselves for the good cause." In fact, as he had two decades before, he quickly left France entirely, not stopping until he reached Ghent in the United Kingdom of Netherlands.

By noon on March 20, 1815, the white flag of the Bourbons had been hauled down from Louis's Tuileries Palace and replaced with the tricolor. An hour later the first of Napoléon's troops entered the capital. It was a small body of troops, a few cavalry, a number of artillerymen—and a coach filled with army cooks.

"Who could defeat Napoléon now?" asked his amazed and jubilant supporters. After all, who but Napoléon could have captured the great city of Paris with just a company of cooks?

Louis XVIII, wearing slippers because of a gout attack, leaves the Tuileries Palace to go into exile.

The Bravest of the Brave

As Napoléon marched north from the Golf Juan-les-Pins and more and more of Louis XVIII's soldiers defected to him, the king had one last hope for retaining power, Marshal Michel Ney.

Ney was a product of the French Revolution and the Napoleonic era. A man of almost no formal education, he was barely literate when he enlisted in the French cavalry. By 1796 the twenty-seven year-old Ney was a general. On May 19, 1804, the day after Napoléon crowned himself emperor, he made Ney marshal of the empire, and in 1805 gave him the title duke of Elchingen, for his victory over the Austrians at that city, which helped make possible Napoléon's triumph at the Battle of Ulm.

Ney fought for Napoléon at Jena, Eylau, and Friedland and later saw service in Spain. When Napoléon invaded Russia in 1812, Ney took command of the Great Army's Third Corps. After Ney distinguished himself at Smolensk and Borodino, Napoléon honored him with the title prince of Moscow. When the French retreated from Moscow, Ney's prowess in battle became even greater as he escaped a Russian trap at Krasnoi. As the Allied noose tightened, Ney fought on but was defeated at Dennewitz and wounded at Leipzig. His military greatness, however, was based less on tactical brilliance—he relied for that on his chief of staff, Baron Antoine-Henri Jomini, who deserted to the Allies in 1813—than on a fierce personal courage. It was no wonder Ney was known as the bravest of the brave.

When the Allies invaded France itself, Ney fought on, but finally he was one of the marshals who called on the emperor to abdicate. As Napoléon returned from Elba, Ney was in the service of the Bourbon dynasty.

Michel Ney strikes a dramatic pose in this painting. An avid supporter of Napoléon, Ney would eventually reject him when he thought Napoléon sought too much power.

Possibilities of Peace

Napoléon's previous wars had cost the European continent two decades of almost ceaseless conflict. The Allies could not believe that Napoléon would settle for merely ruling France once more; they believed he would try to reconquer Europe.

The duke of Wellington wrote to the British foreign secretary Lord Castlereagh on March 26, "Bonaparte and the French nation will not allow [Europe] to remain at peace. . . . It is the desire for war, particularly in the army, which has brought Bonaparte back, and has formed for him any party, and has given him any success."

But Napoléon did want peace—or at least he pretended to. He knew that he was totally outgunned and outmanned by his enemies and their anticipated 700,000 man force. One of the few popular measures Louis XVIII had undertaken was the abolition of the blood tax of conscription. That meant that Napoléon was inheriting an army of just 125,000 soldiers, including 28,000 cavalry. He quickly called up another 12,000 officers and 85,000 enlisted men who had been on leave, in the reserves, or in retirement. In just ten weeks Napoléon had a total force of 250,000 in active service and 220,000 in reserve. In June he would finally feel secure enough politically to begin the conscription of 46,000 recruits—but by that time he was already marching across the Belgian border.

Yet as he built up his army, he also displayed a more moderate and tolerant Napoléon than had ever before existed. He abolished slavery and censorship. He promised more freedom and a new constitution. He handed out pensions and met with thousands of his subjects. To show his new, more conservative side, Napoléon, a former agnostic, even went to mass each Sunday. But he was also up to his old tricks in rigging a referendum, or general election, to legitimize his return to power. When the results were announced on June 1, the totals—1,532,357 in favor to just 4,802 against—were laughably fictional.

Adding to the Allies' belief that Napoléon was an unrestrained warmonger, a veritable mad dog, were the actions of his brother-in-law, Joachim Murat, still the king of Naples. On hearing that Napoléon had escaped from Elba, he rashly declared war on Austria and began marching up the Italian peninsula on a war of conquest.

It was just the beginning of bloodshed—and disaster.

CHAPTER THREE

The Battles of Ligny and Quatre Bras

N apoléon faced two choices in preparing for war. The first was to wait for the Allies to invade France and then to defeat them as they advanced on Paris. Since he had tried this in 1814, and it had failed, he chose the second approach: to attack. Ultimately, the Allies would have 794,000 troops in arms against him—250,000 under Wellington and Blücher, 344,000 under Prince Schwarzenberg and 200,000 under Alexander I of Russia.

On June 7, 1815, Napoléon told France that he would "soon be leading the children of the nation into battle, *pour la patrie* [for the sake of the nation]. We—the Army and I—shall do our duty . . . and you must be prepared to die rather than survive and see France degraded and dishonored."

Napoléon's plan hinged on moving quickly and surprising his numerically superior enemies. He would try to keep them from joining together, for if they did his cause was surely lost, so that he could defeat one and then the other. If he could do this, he might curb Austria and Russia's appetite for war and ensure his survival on the French throne.

Napoléon had but one chance to win against the forces of a Europe united against him. He could afford no mistakes.

The French Command

The portion of the French army Napoléon chose to employ against Wellington and Blücher was known as the Armée du Nord (Army of the North). It was composed of 122,652 men and

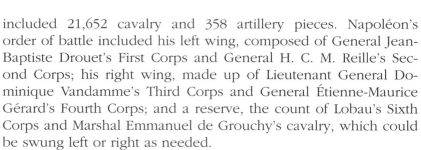

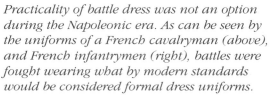

Practicality of battle dress was not an option during the Napoleonic era. As can be seen by the uniforms of a French cavalryman (above), and French infantrymen (right), battles were fought wearing what by modern standards would be considered formal dress uniforms.

included 21,652 cavalry and 358 artillery pieces. Napoléon's order of battle included his left wing, composed of General Jean-Baptiste Drouet's First Corps and General H. C. M. Reille's Second Corps; his right wing, made up of Lieutenant General Dominique Vandamme's Third Corps and General Étienne-Maurice Gérard's Fourth Corps; and a reserve, the count of Lobau's Sixth Corps and Marshal Emmanuel de Grouchy's cavalry, which could be swung left or right as needed.

Napoléon faced a shortage of able military leaders. He could have turned to his brother-in-law, Joachim Murat, who had been defeated in Italy and had fled to France, but in 1813 and 1814 Murat had betrayed Napoléon and the emperor was unable to forgive his treason. He ordered the able Murat to remain inactive at an estate in eastern France.

The Sepoy General

Unlike Napoléon, Great Britain's duke of Wellington was neither particularly magnetic nor beloved by his troops, but he was highly dependable and respected.

Born in Ireland in 1769 as Arthur Wellesley, Wellington entered the British army in 1787. After brief service in Holland he traveled to India, where he distinguished himself both militarily and politically. He remained in India until 1805, when he returned to Europe and became involved in campaigns in northern Germany and in Denmark before being elected to the House of Commons. In 1808 he took command of a division of troops and successfully fought against France's Marshal Soult in the Iberian Peninsula. For his triumphs, a grateful Parliament awarded him the title duke of Wellington and a prize of a half-million pounds sterling.

After Napoléon abdicated the first time, Wellington became Great Britain's ambassador to Paris. While Wellington could see the weakness of Louis XVIII's regime, he thought Napoléon's escape from Elba would fail utterly. Napoléon "has acted upon false or no information, and the king will destroy him without difficulty and in a short period of time," Wellington mistakenly wrote.

For his part, Napoléon also underestimated Wellington, scornfully dismissing him as a mere "Sepoy general," a reference to his service in India as the commander of an army made up of sepoys, or native Indian soldiers. While Wellington was not a great master of strategy, he was solid on defense. He also had the respect of his men, and he was fearless in battle. Said one of his officers, "We would rather see his long nose in the fight than a reinforcement of ten thousand men any day."

What the duke of Wellington lacked in inspiration or strategy, he made up for in personal steadiness and bravery.

As chief of staff, Napoléon chose Nicholas-Jean de Dieu Soult, who had served as Louis XVIII's minister of war. Aside from Soult's Bourbon sympathies, he was an odd choice for chief of staff. Napoléon, after all, had once said of Soult: "He is much better at saying where any army should go, than in actually knowing what to do once it was there." It was a decision that would come back to haunt the emperor.

Marching Toward Waterloo

From June 7 on, French security was tight. No word of Napoléon's lightning strike against Wellington and Blücher was to be allowed to leak out and alert his enemies. Even French fishing boats were forbidden to leave port. Napoléon himself left Paris at 3:00 on the morning of June 12. The attack was rolling forward.

It began with a series of stumbles. First, the commander of the Imperial Guard, Marshal Adolphe Mortier, was crippled by a severe case of sciatica and had to be replaced by his chief of staff, General Antoine Drouot, thus weakening even further Napoléon's already mediocre command staff.

Even more ominous was that Soult failed to communicate properly with Napoléon's corps commanders. It was customary to send out several couriers with the same message to ensure that at least one got through in a timely fashion. Soult, however, sent out just one messenger for each French corps commander. The messenger who was to communicate orders to Vandamme's Third Corps to spearhead the entire advance at 2:30 A.M. failed to reach his camp until 5:00 A.M. When the messenger finally arrived, Vandamme could not be found. An officer was sent out to look for him, but his horse fell on top of him and broke the rider's leg. When Vandamme returned to his headquarters, there was now no one to tell him of Soult's orders. It was only when the count of Lobau's Sixth Corps came marching up behind him that Vandamme learned he was supposed to be leading the invasion of Belgium.

It was a sad omen of the lack of communications and coordination that would haunt Napoléon's forces throughout the entire Waterloo campaign.

Treason

Vandamme's inactivity caused Napoléon's advance to be thrown into utter confusion. Vandamme was to have seized the city of Charleroi at 10:00 A.M., but when Napoléon reached the city at noon, Vandamme was nowhere in sight. In fact, he would not reach Charleroi until 3:00 P.M.

Napoléon was already in a foul mood. On the way to Charleroi he had been informed that one of his ablest generals, Lieutenant General Louis-Auguste de Bourmont, along with two of his officers, had defected to the Prussians. Bourmont had left behind a note explaining that he did not "want to help establish

Napoléon's Chief of Staff

For the crucial post of chief of staff in his upcoming invasion of Belgium, Napoléon needed an officer of tremendous skills. He would have preferred that the post go to Marshal Alexandre Berthier, his former chief of staff. That appointment was not to be, and how Napoléon replaced Berthier seriously affected the outcome of the Battle of Waterloo.

Berthier, tired of strife and merely wishing to live in retirement, refused to join Napoléon at Elba. Napoléon had been severely disappointed but would have readily welcomed his old friend back. Berthier, however, left France as soon as Napoléon returned from Elba. At Bamberg in Germany on June 1, the marshal was killed when he fell from an open window. Whether he fell accidentally, jumped, or was pushed remains a mystery.

To replace the able Berthier, Napoléon chose Marshal Nicholas-Jean de Dieu Soult, the duke of Dalmatia, and until recently Louis XVIII's minister of war. Although Soult's loyalties were in question, he was an able soldier and had fought bravely on the Iberian Peninsula against the British in the Peninsular War, where his enemies had nicknamed him the duke of Damnation. Yet Soult was inexperienced in the role of chief of staff and soon proved that as he failed to coordinate critical issues of communication during the French invasion of Belgium.

Further, his appointment as chief of staff made him unavailable for command of the Armée du Nord's left wing against Wellington. Instead, Napoléon named Marshal Michel Ney to that command. Ney had just arrived in Belgium and was ill-informed about the nature of the forces he commanded and about Napoléon's strategic ideas.

The combination of Soult as chief of staff and Ney as commander of the left wing was a prescription for disaster.

a bloody despotism [dictatorship] in France that would lead to the downfall of the country."

Bourmont had reassured his former comrades that "you will not see me joining the Allies. I shall not give them any information capable of harming the French Army, which I dearly love, and to which I shall always feel deeply attached." But as soon as he was in Prussian hands, he began revealing military secrets. Luckily for the French, the Prussians stupidly paid little attention to what Bourmont told them. By the time Blücher's command was informed of the situation, Napoléon was in control of Charleroi and marching toward Brussels.

Ney and Grouchy Take Command

In Charleroi at 3:30 that afternoon, Napoléon, was surprised by the arrival of Marshal Ney, who he presumed was still in France. The emperor saw Ney's arrival as an opportunity to restructure

Napoléon promoted Emmanuel de Grouchy from commander of the cavalry to commander of the army's right wing during the Battle of Waterloo.

his chaotic command. He gave Ney command of his army's left wing, while promoting Emmanuel de Grouchy from command of the cavalry to leadership of the army's right wing.

Ney's mission would be to advance on Brussels. Standing between him and that city was Wellington's Anglo-Dutch army. Grouchy would move on Fleurus and Sombreffe and engage Blücher's Prussian forces.

Napoléon would soon have cause to regret his decision, for it created even greater dissension in the French ranks. Grouchy's new subordinates, Vandamme and Gérard, considered him unfit for his new command because he was a veteran cavalryman who had never before commanded infantry, and they openly argued against Grouchy. Ney positively loathed Napoléon's chief of staff, Marshal Soult. The two men had served together in Spain, where in a disagreement over strategy Ney had flat-out refused to supply troops for Soult.

Ney was a valiant soldier and an inspiration to his men, but he was weak on strategy. Napoléon recognized this shortcoming. He ridiculed Ney as "brave and nothing more," saying he was "good for leading 10,000 men in battle, but other than that, he was a real blockhead."

The Army of the Low Countries

The 102,500-man Anglo-Dutch army facing Ney was also plagued by its own dissension. King William I of the United Kingdom of Netherlands insisted that his inexperienced twenty-two-year-old son, William, the prince of Orange, be named to command this army. Such an unqualified appointment would have spelled certain disaster for the Anglo-Dutch force, since Napoléon's military genius could easily outmaneuver such an untrained commander.

Common sense eventually prevailed, and the duke of Wellington assumed overall command of the army, but the prince of Orange was given command of the 37,500-man First Corps, consisting of two British and three Dutch divisions. The prince's inexperience, however, was not the only problem facing Wellington's command of the Dutch forces. Many of the troops were French sympathizers who had previously served under Napoléon and might very well desert in the heat of battle. Complicating the matter even further was Dutch war minister, General Janssens, who had fought the British in Java and South Africa and still harbored a healthy dislike for his new allies.

Aside from the prince of Orange's First Corps the remainder of Wellington's forces consisted of Lieutenant General Rowland Hill's Second Corps, made up of one German and four English

divisions; Lieutenant General Uxbridge's Cavalry Corps, composed of seven English, one Hanoverian, one Brunswick, and two Dutch brigades; and the Artillery and Service Corps, consisting of thirty English brigades, thirteen Belgian-Dutch brigades, and sappers and miners who specialized in trench digging and mine laying, respectively.

Wellington had a total of 258 cannons at his command, 180 in the English brigades, and 78 held by the Belgian-Dutch forces.

The Army of the Lower Rhine

Prussian marshal Gebhard von Blücher's Army of the Lower Rhine consisted of 141,900 men, supplemented by 304 cannons.

The bulk of his army was divided into four corps, each consisting of four infantry divisions and one cavalry division: Lieutenant General Hans Ernst Karl von Zieten's First Corps of 32,000 men; Major General Ludwig von Pirch's Second Corps of 34,200 men; Lieutenant General Johann Adolf von Thielmann's Third Corps of 31,200 men; and General Friedrich Wilhelm von Bülow's Fourth Corps of 36,000 men.

On paper Blücher's was a formidable army, but it had major flaws. Only 74,800 of these soldiers were regular army troops; the rest were hastily assembled and ill-trained forces. In the eighteenth century King Frederick the Great's Royal Prussian Army was the model of all European armies, but after his death in 1786 it had declined rapidly. In 1806 it suffered humiliating defeats by Napoléon at Jena and Auerstedt. And Blücher's Saxon forces were hardly more reliable. At the Battle of Leipzig in 1813, six thousand Saxons had deserted to the French. In Belgium on May 2, 1815, two Saxon brigades threatened to mutiny. Blücher ordered them disarmed, burned their regimental banners, and shot seven of their officers.

(Above) This Prussian light-infantryman is shown equipped with a musket. A musket is loaded by first ramming a gunpowder charge down the barrel of the weapon, and then ramming in a musket ball. Due to the length of time involved in this process, muskets were of little use in close combat. The long bayonet attached to the musket became the primary weapon whenever infantrymen engaged in hand-to-hand fighting. (Right) The Prussian cavalryman shown wields a saber, the weapon of choice for most cavalrymen. Unlike swords, which were used for slashing and stabbing opponents, the saber, with its curved, razor-sharp edge, was designed mainly for slashing.

The Allied Plan

The Allies—the British, Dutch, Prussians, Saxons, Russians, and Austrians—had planned to gather together to invade France and overthrow Napoléon. Wellington would move south toward Mons and Cambrai. Blücher would advance toward Charleroi and Maubeuge. They would be assisted by 150,000 Russians driving west from Koblenz in Germany toward Thionville, Metz, and Nancy in France. Two hundred thousand Austrians under Prince Schwarzenberg were massing on the east bank of the Rhine between the Swiss border and the city of Worms.

Any good military commander, however, prepares alternate plans of action. Wellington planned for an initial French move but guessed wrong about where it would come and how. He discounted an invasion at Charleroi because the French had earlier torn up their roads on their side of the border near that city. He guessed that the French would come to the west of Brussels to cut the Allies off from the Belgian ports on the English Channel. Wellington also believed that Napoléon would try to sweep around the Allies' flanks and envelop their entire force. Napoléon, after all, had employed this strategy thirty times in his career—but always when he had superior forces.

In 1815 Napoléon was outnumbered nearly two to one. In such cases as at Rivoli in 1797 and at Leipzig in 1813, he had switched his strategy, massing his force and thrusting into the very center of the enemy. Then he had collapsed the forces at their center and by the very shock of his blow caused panic in their ranks and crumbled their entire defense. It was this center-thrust strategy, and not the sweep that Wellington envisioned, that Napoléon would now use. It posed high risks, but when outnumbered, any strategy is uncertain.

Charleroi and Gilly

Despite receiving clear intelligence reports that Napoléon had massed 100,000 men along the Belgian border, neither Wellington nor Blücher did anything to respond or to coordinate their activities.

Napoléon's Armée du Nord had easily dislodged Prussian general von Zieten from Charleroi. Zieten, following Blücher's orders, retreated slowly toward Fleurus to protect the mass of the Prussian army that was gathering around Sombreffe.

The Prussians had ten thousand infantry in the Fleurus woods near Gilly. Napoléon ordered Grouchy to attack the Prussians as soon as he received reinforcements from Vandamme. However, Vandamme did not arrive until 5:00 P.M. He then wasted nearly another hour arguing with Grouchy over whether the marshal could issue him orders, for he had not received Napoléon's orders placing Grouchy in command of the right wing.

The Duchess of Richmond's Ball

The new war against Napoléon was not only a momentous military and political event, it was also a great social occasion. Many members of the British nobility had come to Brussels to be on hand for the planned Anglo-Dutch invasion of France. Among them was the duchess of Richmond, who had hired a great hall at 9, Rue des Centres for a ball honoring Wellington's forces. One hundred seventy-five invitations were extended for the festivities which would be held on the evening of June 15, 1815.

Throughout the evening elegant carriages carrying even more elegant officers and their ladies arrived. As the couples danced, word of Napoléon's advance had reached Brussels. Not wishing to cause alarm, the duke of Wellington kept his promise to attend the ball, arriving just after midnight. Even before his entrance, however, the rumors had reached the ball. The duke and duchess of Richmond's daughter, Lady Georgiana Lennox, immediately asked Wellington if the rumors were true. He admitted they were and also told her that his army would be on the march that day. Lady Georgiana could not keep a secret, and soon the entire gathering knew a great battle was approaching.

Still Wellington remained at the ball, planning the details of his army's advance amidst the glamour and elegance of a glittering social event.

Finally, Napoléon could stand this inactivity no longer. He hurried to where Grouchy and Vandamme were arguing. Totally frustrated with their bickering, he took personal command of the battle. At 6:00 P.M. on June 15 French artillery and infantry moved forward, and the Prussians fell back in disarray.

Ligny

Blücher was never a great strategist, and his first move of the Waterloo campaign was monstrously poor. The original Allied battle plan, adopted on May 3, called for Blücher to assemble three of his corps at Sombreffe, while Wellington moved his army to meet him. Blücher, however, had not taken into account how fast Napoléon was moving toward him. No sooner had the Prussians reached Sombreffe, than the advancing French would be coming down at them full force. The Prussians would be woefully unprepared to meet them.

Napoléon reached the front to face the Prussians at 11:00 A.M. on June 16. Napoléon had little knowledge of either the terrain or of Blücher's positions, so he slowed his army's advance significantly. He would soon strike with 58,000 infantry, 12,500 cavalry, and 210 cannons. Napoléon thought he would be facing only 40,000 Prussians, but while he hesitated, Zieten's, Pirch's, and Thielmann's forces had come together into a force of 76,000 infantry, 8,000 cavalry, and 224 artillery. Luckily for the French, the Prussians were still too spread out to fight effectively.

Wellington had traveled from his headquarters in Brussels to meet Blücher. At 1:00 P.M. the two conferred at Brye, just behind the Prussian front line. It was an almost pointless meeting. No strategy was agreed on, and Wellington soon returned to his army.

By 2:00 P.M. Napoléon realized he would be facing Blücher's entire army. He knew he needed reinforcements, specifically Ney, who he thought should have captured Quatre Bras, twenty miles outside of Brussels. If Ney could return by 6:00 P.M. he could crush Blücher's army, perhaps destroying as much as two-thirds of it. He sent Ney a message urging his return but added that if Blücher was "overthrown first, then His Majesty [Napoléon] will maneuver in your direction so as to assist you in your operations. . . ." Ney interpreted this to mean he should remain at Quatre Bras.

Napoléon began his attack at 2:30 P.M. As thousands of men battled on the front lines, communications on both sides still left a great deal to be desired. General Drouet was so confused by the conflicting orders he received that day from Napoléon and Marshal Ney that his forces spent most of the day marching back and forth and aiding neither Napoléon nor Ney. On the Prussian side, General Bülow failed to march just six miles in twenty-four hours to aid Blücher.

With a heavy rain now falling, Napoléon ordered a final assault on Blücher to begin at 8:00 P.M. Napoléon's elite Imperial Guard attacked Ligny from both the east and west. Grouchy's cavalry swept down between Tongrinelle and Boignée. The fighting was horrible. The seventy-two-year-old Blücher personally led a cavalry counterattack, but his horse was shot out from under him. Knocked unconscious, he was barely rescued from French captivity.

The Prussians retreated at 9:00 P.M. They had lost 18,772 men and 21 cannons. The French suffered 13,721 casualties.

Napoléon's victory could have been far greater if he had moved more quickly into battle or had had Ney or Drouet's assistance—or had even committed into battle the 10,000 reserves of Lobau's Sixth Corps. Although severely beaten, the Prussians were by no means destroyed as a fighting force.

Summarized Blücher, "We have taken a few knocks and we shall have to hammer out the dents."

Quatre Bras

Ney had left Charleroi in command of Napoléon's left wing but with no clear idea of what to do with it. Only later would he receive any direction from Napoléon. Ney first headed toward Gosselies, eventually capturing it from the Prussians. Thinking he

Blücher's horse is shot out from under him during fierce fighting with Napoléon's troops. Blücher narrowly escaped capture.

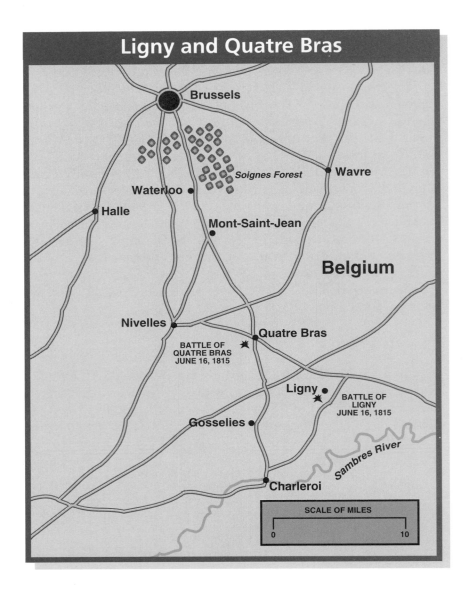

Ligny and Quatre Bras

Brussels

Soignes Forest

Wavre

Waterloo

Halle

Mont-Saint-Jean

Belgium

Nivelles

Quatre Bras

BATTLE OF
QUATRE BRAS
JUNE 16, 1815

Ligny

BATTLE OF
LIGNY
JUNE 16, 1815

Gosselies

Sambres River

Charleroi

SCALE OF MILES

0   10

would encounter only Prussians that day, he came across an un-expected enemy at Quatre Bras: a portion of Wellington's forces.

This encounter was not planned by Wellington either. On hearing that the French were moving rapidly across the border, Wellington had ordered General Constant, chief of the Dutch general staff, to evacuate Quatre Bras and to concentrate his forces at Nivelles.

Had Constant done so, the road to Brussels would have been left totally open to Napoléon. On the grounds that Wellington must have been acting on bad intelligence, Constant purposely chose to ignore Wellington's direct order. His act of insubordina-tion helped change the entire course of the campaign.

Yet, while the British still occupied Quatre Bras, they did not do so in force. Early on the morning of June 16, only 4,000 men held Quatre Bras. As late as 9:00 A.M. only 6,000 soldiers and 8 guns were there under the command of the prince of Orange. Ney had 20,000 men and 50 guns and could have easily overwhelmed the defenders but did not know what to do. Awaiting orders from Napoléon, he did nothing. If he had moved against the prince of Orange, he could possibly have swept the Dutch aside, shattered Anglo-Dutch morale, and driven all the way to Brussels.

Not until 11:00 A.M. would Ney, tired of waiting for Napoléon's instructions, issue his first set of marching orders. And not until 2:00 P.M. would Reille's Second Corps make the first tentative French advances. Still only 8,000 British troops opposed Reille's 20,000. It appeared that despite his late start Reille might carry the day, but at 3:00 P.M. Wellington personally arrived with reinforcements, and Reille retreated. The French attacked once, and it appeared they could still win, but the German duke of Brunswick, Frederick William, arrived with the Brunswick Corps.

During the Battle of Quatre Bras, poor communication between Napoléon and his generals led to unnecessary delays and a complete lack of coordinated effort.

At this point Ney finally attacked. He determined to finish off the Anglo-Dutch forces, once more ordering Reille forward. He also called on Drouet's First Corps of 20,000 men into the battle against Wellington. But Drouet, who had spent the entire day

marching back and forth between Napoléon and Ney without joining either still managed to avoid combat. By mistake Drouet had received a poorly written communication from Ney to move against Blücher. He attempted to carry out the order but reported to Saint-Amand instead of to Wagnelee, where Napoléon, who needed reinforcements there, had actually ordered him. When Drouet got to Wagnelee, but before he engaged the Prussians, he received orders from Ney to march back to Quatre Bras. In the meantime his presence in the wrong sector was misinterpreted by other French as an enemy advance. To thwart this supposed attack, Napoléon diverted some of his troops to where Drouet was and away from the attack on Blücher. As these troops advanced, Drouet obeyed Ney's orders and withdrew. But he arrived at Quatre Bras too late to make a difference, and while Drouet wasted his entire day Ney had suffered an embarrassing and unnecessary defeat.

At 4:30 P.M. Napoléon ordered Ney to aid him in crushing Blücher. "The fate of France is in your hands," Ney was bluntly told, "so do not hesitate for an instant. . . ." Yet Ney could not even extricate himself from the fierce fighting with Wellington. Aided by the arrival of still more reinforcements, Wellington forced Ney back as far as Frasnes. The French, who that morning could have easily swept aside the Anglo-Dutch forces, suffered forty-seven hundred casualties while their enemy lost just forty-three hundred.

It was but one of a series of critical missed opportunities for the French.

CHAPTER FOUR

Waterloo: The French Attack

The Prussians had suffered a severe reversal at Ligny, yet their morale remained high. They seemed more ready for renewed combat than a recently vanquished army should have. After losing at the Battle of Étoges in 1814, Blücher had not been ready to fight again for five days. Now, even though he had been seriously injured, his army seemed ready for anything. The French, on the other hand, seemed sluggish and unmotivated.

Nineteenth-century historian William Siborne in his *History of the War in France and Belgium in 1815* remarked:

> The contrast between the circumstances of the two armies during the night was very striking; for whilst the victors were indulging in perfect repose, the vanquished were completely on the alert, seizing every possible advantage which the extraordinary inactivity of their enemies afforded during the precious hours of darkness; and never, perhaps, did a defeated army extricate itself from its difficulties with so much adroitness and order, or retire from a hard-fought field with so little diminution [decrease] of its moral force. The Prussian commander [Blücher], completely *hors de combat* [disabled], was carried to Gentinnes, about six miles in rear of Ligny, but from the moment his fall became known, his chief of staff Count Gneisenau undertook the direction of affairs.

The Prussian Reaction

As the Prussian retreat proceeded, Blücher, in great pain, regained consciousness. He not only got out of bed but mounted a horse for a better command of the situation. He resolved not just

to avoid the destruction of his own army, but to destroy Napoléon's. To his just beaten forces went the orders: "I shall immediately lead you against the enemy;—we shall beat him, because it is our duty to do so."

Blücher's goal was to keep in contact with Wellington and to join up with him as quickly as possible. The French, however, failed to recognize the Prussians' strategy. Instead, they incorrectly guessed that Blücher would simply retreat along his supply lines. At 4:00 in the morning of June 17, French cavalry leader Lieutenant Colonel Claude-Pierre Pajol, who had been ordered to reconnoiter, or survey, the area, sent word back to Napoléon that the Prussians were in a disorderly retreat toward Namur. Two hours later Napoléon awoke and read Pajol's report. It lulled him into a sense of false security. He thought he could safely and leisurely set his forces upon Wellington's, with little worry of Blücher's joining the battle and tipping the balance against him.

In spite of a painful fall, Gebhard Leberecht von Blücher was determined to face Napoléon and revenge his defeat. His timely arrival at Waterloo would allow Wellington to win the battle.

Wellington's Strategy

At 7:30 A.M. a British cavalry patrol informed Wellington of Blücher's defeat. Wellington instantly realized that Napoléon's armies would now be bearing down on him. He further saw that Quatre Bras was not the ideal place to make a stand against the reinforced French. Despite the fact that a retreat would make his hard-fought victory of the day before look like a defeat, Wellington ordered his men toward Brussels. He said: "I suppose in England they will say we have been licked. I can't help it; as [the Prussians] have gone back, we must go too." The commander of the British Fifth Division, Lieutenant General Thomas Picton, could barely control his contempt for Wellington's orders. At 10:00 A.M. British forces would begin concentrating on the heights of Mont-Saint-Jean, just south of the village of Waterloo.

While Blücher and Wellington swung into action, Napoléon ate a leisurely breakfast, taking time out to have Soult send a critical letter to Ney:

> His Majesty was grieved to learn that you did not succeed yesterday; the divisions acted in isolation and you therefore sustained losses. If the corps of Counts Reille and d'Erlon [Drouet] had been together, not a soldier of the English corps that came to attack you would have escaped; if Count d'Erlon had executed the movement on St. Amand ordered by the emperor, the Prussian army would have been totally destroyed and we should perhaps have taken 30,000 prisoners.

Napoléon further informed Ney of Blücher's alleged retreat to Namur and ordered Ney to try again to dislodge Wellington from Quatre Bras.

Napoléon should have given his own troops orders to do something—anything. They could have moved against Blücher; they did not, and as every hour passed following Ligny the sting of defeat left the Prussian army, and their morale improved. Napoléon's troops could have joined Ney to make following his orders easier. Instead, they sat and waited. In midmorning of June 17, Napoléon finally stirred himself, but only to visit his troops and receive their enthusiastic cheers. His generals impatiently waited for some direction.

At 9:00 A.M. Ney received Napoléon's orders. Their tone offended him, and he saw that taking Quatre Bras without reinforcements was still an impossibility. Wellington simply had him outnumbered. He, too, did nothing.

Napoléon Arrives at Quatre Bras

After finishing his grand tour of his troops, Napoléon entered his coach and headed for Quatre Bras. By 1:00 P.M. he had reached Marbais. His troops were having lunch, and Napoléon himself stopped for a quick bite to eat. On the move again toward Quatre Bras, Napoléon was now joined by his Imperial Guard. At 2:00 P.M., just one mile from his destination, Napoléon left his coach and mounted his horse, Desiree. A growing sense of nervousness gripped him. He realized that no military action was happening. He soon came upon Drouet, and seeing that only a rearguard of British troops remained at Quatre Bras, Napoléon screamed, "France has been ruined."

Napoléon ordered his troops to pursue the retreating enemy. As he did, a violent storm broke, making movement difficult. But still the British headed toward Waterloo, with the French trailing behind them.

As Napoléon got Ney's forces moving, ten miles to the east, 33,000 troops under the command of Marshal Grouchy were on a different mission. Napoléon had dispatched Grouchy to determine what Blücher was up to and to pursue him. Grouchy's scouts had discovered that at least a column of Prussians was heading toward Wavre. This struck the marshal as ominous. If Wellington was falling back toward Brussels, Blücher could join the Anglo-Dutch forces. If that happened, the French position would instantly become perilous.

Grouchy sent a message to Napoléon suggesting that "perhaps it may be inferred that one portion is going to join Wellington. . . ." He added that if he saw "the masses of the Prussian army" moving toward Wavre, he would move forward "to separate them from Wellington."

The Unequal Equals

At Waterloo, Napoléon and Wellington faced each other with nearly equal forces. Yet Napoléon clearly expected to roll over his Anglo-Dutch opponents, while the duke feared that same possibility. There were several reasons for such attitudes.

Wellington's army contained a mixed force of British, Dutch, and German soldiers. Barely a third were British, and even most of those soldiers were untried in battle. Wellington pleaded for the experienced veterans of the Peninsular War, but they remained in Great Britain. His forces' loyalties to the Allied cause were equally mixed. Wellington, with typically brutal candor, termed it an "infamous army." The French, on the other hand, were well-tested veterans of Napoléon's many campaigns. In terms of cavalry, Napoléon's cuirassiers, or cavalrymen, clearly outranked Wellington's mounted troops both numerically and in quality.

Napoléon, who had started out as an artillery officer, held a similar advantage in terms of artillery. The French possessed nearly one hundred more guns than the British did, and many of their cannons were huge, twelve-pound guns. The best Wellington could muster were far less powerful nine-pounders.

And among key commanders, despite the flaws of Ney, Soult, and Grouchy, they stood far above the experience of the twenty-two-year-old prince of Orange or of eighteen-year-old Prince Frederick, who held their commands only by virtue of their royal blood.

For the rest of the afternoon Napoléon pursued Wellington, but without success. Meanwhile Blücher arrived at Wavre. Unaware of Blücher's movement toward him, Napoléon paused for the night. "Have all the troops take up positions," he told Drouet, "and we will see what happens tomorrow." The rain continued into the night, creating an ocean of mud so thick and deep that soldiers lost their boots in it.

Wellington's Strategy of Defense

Napoléon set up his headquarters at le Caillou, a farmhouse on the Brussels road just six miles from Wellington's headquarters. Wellington was now operating on a false assumption, believing that he was facing Napoléon's entire army and not realizing that Grouchy was no longer with the emperor. Like Napoléon, Wellington, too, had split his forces, but with a defensive purpose in mind. At Mont-Saint-Jean the duke commanded 68,000 men and 156 cannons. But at Halle, ten miles to the west, Wellington placed 17,000 troops and 30 guns under the command of Prince Frederick of the Netherlands. Wellington was obsessed by the idea that Napoléon would try cutting him off from the English Channel. Frederick's army was an insurance policy against a strategy that Napoléon had no intention of using. Some historians have questioned Wellington's strategy for another reason: if he were to protect one of his flanks, it should have been his opposite one, to prevent Napoléon from permanently separating him from Blücher.

Wellington's main defensive line was north of the Ohain road. His tactics would be of the same sort he had employed so successfully in the Peninsular War. The Anglo-Dutch front row

The farmhouse at le Caillou near Waterloo where Napoléon set up his headquarters to plan his battle strategy.

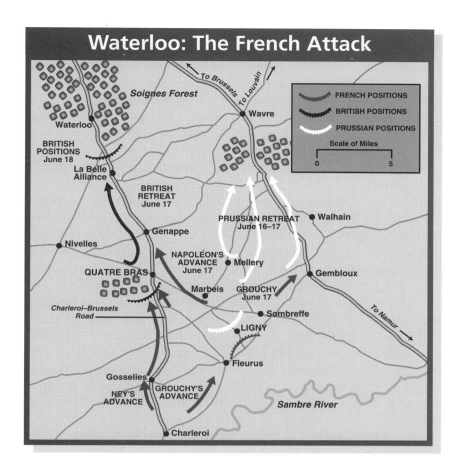

Waterloo: The French Attack

would consist of artillery and infantry, who would bear the first burden of holding off an attack; the second row would be infantry, who would be hidden from the enemy's sight until the front row was unable to respond any further. Then the infantrymen would fire volley after volley to stop the French in their tracks. Held in reserve would be Wellington's cavalry, to be used if a counterattack was in order.

Wellington established several advance outposts: at Hougoumont, la Haye Sainte, Papelotte, la Haye, and Frichermont. Fifteen hundred men under Colonel James Macdonnell and Colonel Saltoun garrisoned, or stationed troops in, an orchard surrounded by walls and hedges at Hougoumont. Within the orchard were a château and several farm buildings.

At la Haye Sainte, in the center of Wellington's front, Major George Baring's Second Battalion of the king's German Legion, two German Nassau battalions, and one brigade barricaded themselves at a farmhouse. Just across the Charleroi road additional troops hid in a gravel pit, waiting for the French attack.

At the outposts of Papelotte, la Haye, and Frichermont, the prince of Saxe-Weimar-Eisenach's brigade dug in to protect Wellington's left wing.

The Morning of the Battle

Napoléon was brimming with confidence as he sat down with his generals for breakfast at 8:00 A.M. on June 18. "The enemy army is numerically superior to ours by almost a quarter," observed Napoléon, unaware that Prince Frederick was at Halle, "yet, we have no less than 90 per cent of the chances in our favor, and not ten against us." But the emperor would soon have reason to doubt his optimism. Ney warned him that the British were assuming defensive positions in the woods. Soult and Reille warned Napoléon of the dangers of frontally attacking the historically tenacious British infantry. Most ominously, Prince Jérôme Bonaparte shared a piece of intelligence he had learned over dinner the previous evening. His waiter had told him that one of Wellington's aides had revealed plans for "a concerted link-up between the British and the Prussians coming from Wavre."

Napoléon dismissed the report as "foolishness," and bragged that "after a battle like Ligny, the joining up of the British and the Prussians is impossible. If my orders are carried out, we will sleep in Brussels tonight." He seemed in no hurry to join Wellington in combat. The assault was originally scheduled to begin at 9:00 A.M.—after his men had breakfasted—but because the rain had not yet ceased, and the mud of the previous evening had only increased, Napoléon gave orders to delay the attack. During the delay, when he could have been dictating instructions to his generals, he toured the battlefield, preferring the cheers of his adoring men to the detailed work of developing

Sketches from the notebook of one of Napoléon's officers show how the men made preparations to camp while in the field.

strategies necessary for victory. Napoléon's newfound indifference to events also manifested itself when he delegated to Ney that afternoon's battlefield command. Napoléon had once likened Michel Ney's military knowledge to that "of the last-joined drummer boy," and based on Ney's inactivity at Quatre Bras, Napoléon's opinion of him had not increased in the last few days. Perhaps, he thought, even a dimwit like Ney could handle a simple forward assault.

Still, there must have been some concern in Napoléon's generally overconfident mind. In response to his brother Jérôme's report, he ordered Colonel Marbot's Seventh Hussars, or cavalry, to protect his army's right flank against a possible Prussian attack near Lasne. Adding to his concern was the inability of the French army to get moving, by now a chronic condition.

At 10 o'clock the previous evening Marshal Grouchy, who was proving remarkably immobile in pursuing Blücher, had sent Napoléon another dispatch, again warning of the possibility of a Wellington-Blücher linkup: "My information is that the Prussians are retreating toward Wavre. If the mass of their forces goes to Wavre, I shall follow to prevent them from reaching Brussels and rejoining Wellington. If their principal forces retreat to Liége, I shall follow them there."

Napoléon had been awakened at 3:00 A.M. and given Grouchy's dispatch. He did not bother to answer it until 10:00 A.M., informing Grouchy that he was about to attack Wellington. He ordered Grouchy to Wavre, "where you should proceed as soon as possible in order to come closer to us and to establish operational liaison with us whilst pressing the enemy before you." Grouchy did not receive this message until 4:00 that afternoon.

Slowly Napoléon's army assembled. Part of the problem was that the mud made artillery movements nearly impossible. It was not until 11:00 A.M. that he issued this Order of Battle:

> Once the whole army is ranged in battle order, at about 1:00 P.M., and when the Emperor gives Marshal Ney the relevant order, the attack will begin in order to capture the village of Mont-St Jean, which is the road junction. To this end, the 12-inch batteries of II and VI Corps will regroup with those of I Corps. These 94 cannon will fire on the troops of Mont St Jean and Count d'Erlon [Drouet] will begin the attack by bringing forward his left wing division, supporting it, according to the circumstances, by the other I Corps divisions. II Corps will advance so as to keep at the level of Count d'Erlon. The sapper companies of I Corps will be ready to entrench themselves immediately at Mont St Jean.

Napoléon would continue his plan of a straight frontal attack. Even if he had wanted to change his strategy to sweeping around Wellington, the mud would have made such an idea impossible.

Still, the main French assault did not proceed until 1:00 P.M. But as it did, Napoléon spotted some activity, far off to the east, near the Bois de Paris (Paris Woods). The emperor sent his aide-de-camp, or military aide, Lieutenant General Simon Bernard, to learn what it was about. When Bernard returned, Napoléon's worst fears were confirmed. Bülow's Fourth Corps of Prussians was slowly moving toward the right French flank. He would have to defeat Wellington before the English and Anglo-Dutch forces united to crush the Grande Armée—a matter of mere hours. And he would have to do it with almost no reserve forces, for he had committed Lobau's Sixth Corps to guard against the Prussians. All Napoléon would have left for a final push against Wellington was his elite Imperial Guard.

Waiting for Grouchy

Accordingly, at 1:15 P.M. Napoléon had Marshal Soult send another message to Grouchy. It was clear that Grouchy would have to quickly return to Napoléon's main forces to prevent disaster. However, the instructions failed to communicate the growing urgency of the situation. Soult betrayed his lack of qualifications to be chief of staff when he wrote to Grouchy:

> Monsieur le Maréchal [Marshal], You wrote to the Emperor this morning at 6 A.M. that you would march on Sart-à-Walhain. You were planning therefore to go to Corbais and Wavre. This movement is in accordance with His Majesty's dispositions [arrangements] which have been communicated to you. However, the Emperor orders me to tell you that you must always manoeuvre in our direction and seek to come closer to us in order to join us before any corps can come between us. I do not indicate any direction to you. It is for you to see the point where we are, to regulate yourself in consequence and to bind our communications, as well as always to be in a position to fall upon any enemy troops which would seek to worry [harass] our right flank, and to crush them. At this time, the battle is engaged on the line at Waterloo.

Soult, however, then added the following, only slightly more urgent, words: "The enemy center is at Mont St Jean, so do manoeuvre to join our right." Then Napoléon finally ordered him to get to the point, "P.S. A letter just intercepted says that General Bülow is going to attack our right flank. We think that we can perceive this corps on the heights of St Lambert. Do not lose one moment, therefore, in coming closer to us, joining us and in crushing Bülow whom you will catch red-handed."

As Napoléon dictated these words, his artillery began its bombardment of Wellington's line. Off beyond Wavre, Grouchy could hear the cannon booming. General Étienne-Maurice

The Defensive Square

If cavalry surprised infantry, it could literally cut to pieces the foot soldiers with sabers and lances. However, infantry could turn to a highly effective defensive tactic: the square.

Simply put, the idea behind a square was the same one as circling the wagons in the American West. Caught out in the open, infantry would group into a square position, with each side of the square composed of two or three lines of soldiers firing as rapidly as they could at the advancing cavalry. Reinforcement could often be found inside the square, ready to pour more firepower on the attackers. In this manner the cavalry would quickly find its advantage destroyed.

However, for cavalry supported by artillery a square made an inviting target for the gunners, who would fire cannonballs into the densely packed mass of troops. At that point the square would dissolve, and the cavalry would swing into action again. Squares were also at a disadvantage if attacked on one side by other infantry, as three-quarters of the firepower would be aimed in the wrong direction.

Because of these factors, an infantry unit exposed to attack might slip in and out of a square position several times during an engagement.

French cavalry charge British troop squares at Waterloo. Wellington can be seen at midground, right. Rockets can be seen streaking through the smoke-filled sky at left, center.

Emmanuel de Grouchy

Born in Paris in 1766, Marshal Grouchy, like Ney, was a career army officer. An aristocrat by birth he nonetheless faithfully served the forces of the French Revolution as an accomplished cavalryman. In 1793 he helped put down a royalist uprising in France's Vendée region, and from 1796 to 1797 he served in France's Army of Ireland. He returned to France and fought against the Austrians and Russians before being captured at the Battle of Novi Ligure in August 1799. The French secured his release, and from 1801 onward Napoléon used Grouchy in a series of important military and political posts. Unlike Ney, when Louis XVIII returned to France, Grouchy was denied any military command or even an audience with Louis. But when Napoléon escaped from Elba, Napoléon promoted him to marshal, the last marshal of the empire ever created.

Although Grouchy had proven to be one of France's best cavalry officers, second only to Joachim Murat, before 1815 he had never commanded a mixed force of cavalry, infantry, and artillery. He was clearly over his head in a critical situation.

Gérard excitedly told Grouchy he should join Napoléon in the attack on Wellington. Grouchy refused, feeling that he had earlier been ordered directly by Napoléon to pursue the Prussians by marching on them at Wavre and that he could not willfully disobey the emperor's orders.

Napoléon's new orders—to move to Waterloo—would not reach Grouchy until between 5:00 and 6:00 P.M., when it would be far too late for action.

Blücher's Strategy

Blücher's plan for victory involved having two or three corps move against Napoléon's right flank. Like Napoléon, with Grouchy split off from his main force, and Wellington, as with Prince Frederick at Halle, he did not commit all his forces to the coming struggle. He hedged his bets against an attack by Grouchy by leaving one corps, led by Thielmann, at Wavre. The Fourth Corps would move first against the French, with the Second Corps right behind them. The First Corps would march to the north to directly reinforce Wellington.

While it was only a ten-to-twelve mile march for Blücher's soldiers, it would not be an easy advance. Even under the best of circumstances, the terrain was difficult. No roads or even decent paths marked the route—only streams, dense woods, and fields that had turned into mud. That artillery could have been brought even that distance over that terrain on the morning of June 18 was a remarkable accomplishment for the Prussians and a monument to their grim determination. Complicating the move, however, was a controversial act by Blücher. General von Bülow's spearheading Fourth Corps was actually the farthest away from Waterloo. Some say Blücher and his chief of staff, Lieutenant General Auguste Wilhelm von Gneisenau wanted Fourth Corps to lead the attack because, after the Prussians' rough handling at Ligny, it was the corps in the best shape. In any case, to reach the front of the march, it would have to pass by Zieten's First Corps, Pirch's Second Corps, and Thielmann's Third Corps. Such maneuvering cost the Prussians precious time and needlessly slowed their progress toward Waterloo.

Yet, at least the Prussians moved. Unlike the French, whose leisurely 9:00 A.M. attack was delayed until 1:00 P.M., Bülow's Fourth Corps began its march at 4:00 A.M. The corps arrived at Saint Lambert between 9:00 A.M. and 11:00 A.M. The remainder of the Prussians were further delayed by a fire that broke out in Wavre, but they still reached Saint Lambert by noon.

CHAPTER FIVE

"La Garde Recule!"

On June 16 only one commander, Blücher, had tasted defeat. Both Napoléon and Wellington had emerged triumphant. But, ironically, on the eighteenth only Blücher was moving forward with full confidence. He was fully determined to crush his French adversaries and destroy Napoléon once and for all.

Wellington, the victor of Quatre Bras, had made three false assumptions. First, he was unaware that Blücher was marching to his aid. In this matter he was not helped by elements of Blücher's staff who did not trust their English allies and were keeping their frenzied activities secret. Second, Wellington thought Napoléon would attempt to cut him off from the English Channel and detached part of his army to guard against this attack that Napoléon never planned on launching. Third, he did not know that Napoléon had split his own army and that Grouchy was roaming in a seemingly aimless fashion near Wavre. Accordingly, he erroneously thought he was outnumbered by the French and, therefore, assumed a defensive position at Mont-Saint-Jean.

Napoléon, the victor at Ligny, now had a fairly clear view of reality, but it made him increasingly nervous: "This morning we had ninety chances in our favor. Even now we have sixty chances, and only forty against us." With Blücher's army slowly bearing down upon him, Napoléon faced two choices: withdraw to fight again or immediately attack Wellington and defeat him in the handful of hours he had left before Blücher arrived.

Withdrawal had two massive drawbacks. The first was military. If Wellington and Blücher united, there might never be another chance to defeat them separately. And with the Austrians and Russians massing in Germany, the situation would only grow worse.

His political situation was nearly as precarious. France, after more than two decades of war, was simply worn out. Napoléon faced serious opposition at home. If he withdrew, if he retreated, he might face protest and intrigue in France itself, which he could not afford. "Pressed for time by the political unrest in Paris and throughout France, he needed not merely a victory but a brilliant victory," summed up Henry Lachouque in his book, *Waterloo.*

Hougoumont

Although Napoléon's strategy of forcing a breach in Wellington's lines with a massive forward thrust was simple enough, he added a new element to it. At 11:30 A.M. he ordered a diversionary attack on Hougoumont. His hope was that Wellington would divert troops from the portion of the main defensive line to Hougoumont, thus making the French attack on the Anglo-Dutch line easier.

Prince Jérôme Bonaparte's Sixth Division, a component of Reille's Second Corps, led the attack on Hougoumont. Supported by cavalry, his four regiments were at first repulsed by the German Nassau and Hanover troops defending the position, but he

Though this engraving greatly overestimates the numbers of French at Hougoumont, it shows British foot guards attacking and driving back French troops attempting to penetrate by the rear gate.

kept throwing more and more of his troops into the fighting in a desperate bid to seize the château. It was not to be, however. "The farm is well calculated [situated] for defense," noted Colonel Woodford of the Coldstream Guards, one of the British units guarding Hougoumont. "The dwelling-house in the centre was a strong square building, with small doors and windows." The French were hindered further by the six-foot-high walls and gates of the site. At one point Jérôme's men forced their way through the main gate of the château and into its courtyard. But the British fought back fiercely, killing all but one of the invaders, save for a drummer boy who was taken prisoner, and forcing the gate closed against them.

Soon after the gate was closed, Woodford's Coldstream Guards arrived to reinforce Hougoumont's defenders, permanently securing the position. Said Wellington: "You may depend on it, that no troops but the British could have held Hougoumont, and only the best of them at that."

A puzzling aspect of the French units' attack was their failure to use artillery in the assault until very late in the day. Had they bombarded Hougoumont earlier, their chances of taking the château might have increased significantly.

The Main Assault Begins

At 1:20 P.M. the main French assault on Wellington's line began with a volley by eighty cannons, which had massed just to the right of la Belle-Alliance battlefield. Wellington's guns immediately returned their fire. The exchange lasted for about half an hour, and while it raised much noise and dust, the French guns inflicted little serious damage to the Anglo-Dutch line. At 2:00 P.M. the French shelling stopped momentarily, and eighteen thousand of Napoléon's infantry under the command of Ney and Drouet marched forward across the twelve hundred yards that separated the two opposing armies.

At this very beginning of the main French attack, Ney and Drouet committed two major tactical errors. First, the infantry assault should have been immediately preceded by an attack by Napoléon's crack cavalry. Had the cavalry attacked first, Wellington's forces would have been forced to mass into squares in order to protect themselves from the cuirassiers' slashing sabers, thus dramatically reducing the firepower of their muskets. As it was, as the French infantry marched across unharvested fields of rye toward their opponents, a long, deadly line of muskets rose to rain fire down upon them.

Second, Ney and Drouet deployed three-quarters of their advancing forces in an outmoded formation, in division width, rather than in the more modern battalion width. Having infantry advance in such a wide formation—two hundred men across and twenty-

Wellington, in the civilian costume of blue frock coat and cape that would be characteristic of him, gives orders to his staff. Somerset's brigade is charging the enemy in the background.

seven deep—not only made it more difficult for them to maneuver, it also made them even more vulnerable to the enemy's artillery fire by creating a wider target for the enemy gunners.

Despite taking heavy losses, the French moved steadily forward. "No commander was better served by his soldiers," Napoléon would later admiringly write of his forces at Waterloo. Lieutenant General Donzelot's Second Division, aided by a detachment of cavalry, held the extreme right wing of the French assault at Papelotte and la Haye Sainte. In the center were Brigadier General Quiot's First Division and Lieutenant General Marcognet's Third Division. On the extreme left was Lieutenant General Durutte's Fourth Division. Ney and Drouet placed themselves personally at the head of Quiot's forces.

The British Counterattack

The defenders of the outpost at la Haye Sainte held their positions as Durutte swept around them and easily captured Papelotte. In the center, French forces seemed on the verge of overrunning the Allied line, but suddenly Sir Thomas Picton ordered his Fifth Division to attack. Picton was instantly killed by a shot to the temple, but his men swept forward, pushing Donzelot's Second Division back.

Meanwhile, Ney was finally ordering his cavalry into action. But again he was too slow. Wellington's own commander of cavalry, the earl

William Uxbridge, Wellington's brother-in-law and commander of the British cavalry. His prompt action at Waterloo would contribute to Napoléon's defeat.

of Uxbridge, who was also Wellington's brother-in-law, ordered his horsemen to attack before the French cavalry had time to make their presence felt in any meaningful degree. All across the front the British cavalry swept the French back. At Papelotte, Durutte's men withdrew in an orderly fashion, but elsewhere the French infantry were cut to pieces by the British. Uxbridge's forces charged headlong at the French lines, killing the crews of thirty enemy cannons. By now the French had suffered heavy casualties, five thousand in all, including three thousand captured. "The plain had been swept clean," recalled Uxbridge, "and I never saw so joyous a group as [the group around Wellington]. They thought the battle was over."

They were wrong; it was just beginning.

The First Desperate Gamble

Uxbridge's gallant charge had its price: twenty-five hundred dead, wounded, or captured British cavalrymen. Among them was the Second Cavalry Brigade's commander, Sir William Ponsonby. After his horse tripped in the soggy ground, Ponsonby was killed by French lancers.

As this carnage transpired, Napoléon watched. He was all too aware that the Prussians were moving ever closer. Although Napoléon could not know it, Wellington had received word from Bülow that the Prussians would attack at around 4:00 P.M. Making Napoléon even more nervous was a message he received from Grouchy at 3:30 P.M. Written at 11:00 A.M., it indicated that Grouchy was only at Sart-à-Walhain, nine miles from Wavre, and still not in contact with any of Blücher's army. Napoléon would later sarcastically write, "With 34,000 men and 108 cannon, Grouchy found the matchless secret, on 18th June, of finding himself neither on the battlefield of Mont St Jean, nor in Wavre." It was now obvious to the emperor that there was no hope of Grouchy's returning in time to be of help against Blücher.

A bold Napoleonic stroke was in order. In fact, it was overdue. The emperor ordered Ney to take la Haye Sainte, for if the Allies still held that outpost, attacks on Wellington's center were almost doomed to failure.

But before la Haye Sainte could fall, the second piece of Napoléon's strategy would roll into place: a mass cavalry charge of five thousand experienced horsemen, attacking on a frontline of just five hundred yards. It would be one of the fiercest cavalry attacks in history.

Napoléon had wished for the cavalry to assemble carefully and to be supplemented by infantry. Ney, who had previously been so careful, now operated in exactly the opposite manner. While attacking la Haye Sainte, Ney noticed a withdrawal to the rear by Wellington's wounded and the mass of French prisoners

the Anglo-Dutch had already taken. The marshal mistook this movement for a disorganized retreat and determined to take advantage of it. Accordingly, he ordered his cavalry, unsupported by any infantry, to attack immediately.

The Allies met Ney with a bloody welcome. First, Wellington's artillery fired point-blank into the charging cuirassiers. Then, as the French were just thirty yards from the Allied line, musket fire caused even greater havoc. Lieutenant Edward Macready of the British Thirtieth Regiment recalled seeing "helmets falling, cavaliers starting [leaping] from their seats with convulsive springs, . . . horses plunging and rearing in the agonies of fright and pain."

At 4:20 P.M. the first wave of French cavalry had been repulsed. A tense but now optimistic Wellington observed, "The battle is mine; and if the Prussians arrive soon, there will be an end to the war."

Ney, still forgetting to bring his infantry into the attack, was obsessed with overrunning the Allied line. Following another French artillery barrage, he ordered a second French cavalry charge to surge forward. This time the riders' progress was slowed not only by murderous fire, but also from having to ride over the bodies of hundreds of their fallen comrades and the carcasses of horses. At one point the French overran a large portion of Wellington's artillery. It was here that Napoléon's observation that the attack had come too early again proved true. Ney should

Two vast armies (eighty thousand men on each side) engage in fierce hand-to-hand combat. Bloodied and confused, Napoléon's soldiers at the Battle of Waterloo would be defeated.

The Battle of Waterloo

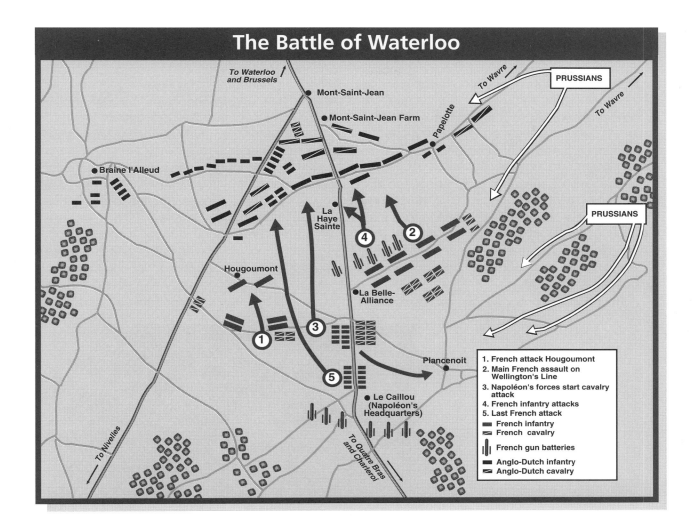

Legend:
1. French attack Hougoumont
2. Main French assault on Wellington's Line
3. Napoléon's forces start cavalry attack
4. French infantry attacks
5. Last French attack

- French infantry
- French cavalry
- French gun batteries
- Anglo-Dutch infantry
- Anglo-Dutch cavalry

Map labels: To Waterloo and Brussels; Mont-Saint-Jean; Mont-Saint-Jean Farm; Braine l'Alleud; La Haye Sainte; Hougoumont; La Belle-Alliance; Plancenoit; Le Caillou (Napoléon's Headquarters); To Nivelles; To Quatre Bras and Charleroi; Papelotte; To Wavre; PRUSSIANS; PRUSSIANS

have been prepared either to haul the Anglo-Dutch guns back or to disable them. Neither action was taken. Instead, Wellington's men forced the French back. "Had the guns been spiked [rendered useless by having large nails driven into their fuse holes]," wrote military historian J.F.C. Fuller in *The Decisive Battles of the Western World*, "which could have been done with headless nails and hammers, the next great [French] cavalry assault would almost have certainly succeeded."

Both sides were taking heavy casualties. At 5:00 P.M. the French infantry finally attacked. Napoléon, watching the battle from la Belle-Alliance, marveled at the bravery of his men. On the opposing side, even in the face of the worst of the French attack, the British reacted with remarkable courage, as well. At one point during that afternoon's French cavalry attack, Wellington rode up to the Fifth Brigade's Major General Colin Halkett. He asked Halkett how his forces were faring. Halkett, who ultimately would take eleven separate French charges, responded,

Napoléon's Health

One of the great controversies surrounding the Battle of Waterloo revolves around Napoléon's physical state. He was just forty-six, and commentators both on Elba and in France following his return remarked on his excellent health. Historian Jacques Champagne in Chalfont's *Waterloo* points to Napoléon's ability during the crucial ninety-six hours of Waterloo to remain in the saddle for thirty-seven hours and to sleep for just twenty hours and contends that the emperor "can hardly be said to be in a bad state of health."

But many others claim he was in ill health at Waterloo. Even Jacques Champagne admits that during the battle Napoléon suffered from a "very bad spasmodic cough," stomach pains, and hemorrhoids. Other historians even contended he may also have been suffering from cystitis, hepatitis, and venereal disease. Lord Chalfont himself contends that Napoléon suffered from the "appalling pains of the [intestinal] cancer which was eventually to kill him."

Such intense pain may have caused Napoléon's lack of interest in vital details, and his slowness of action and may have helped change the course of history.

Historians wonder just how much Napoléon's judgment was affected by the pain of worsening stomach cancer. Normally precise and quick, he delayed action and made poor decisions during the Battle of Waterloo.

"My Lord, we are dreadfully cut up, can you not relieve us for awhile?" Wellington replied with a single word, "Impossible." "Very well," said Halkett, "we'll stand till the last man falls."

The Prussians Arrive

At times Wellington's situation was desperate. With just a heavier push by the French, he would be overrun. "It was the most desperate business I was ever in," Wellington would later admit. "I never took so much trouble about any battle, I was never so near being beat."

Ney had begged Napoléon for reinforcements, but Napoléon refused. Napoléon, who still had the sixteen battalions of his Imperial Guard in reserve, stormed, "Troops? Where does he expect me to find them? Am I to make them?"

But as Wellington fought on, the Prussians under Blücher were finally at the scene in force and about to begin their attack on the mass of Napoléon's forces. At 7:00 P.M. Napoléon could hear the cannon of Zieten's First Corps. The Prussians were bearing down on him at full force. The chances for a French victory were dwindling to almost nothing. A careful retreat could have preserved the Armée du Nord to fight again another day, but instead Napoléon pressed ahead with one last, desperate gamble. He threw his last reserves, the faithful Old Guard, a division of the Imperial Guard, into the battle. As he did so, to bolster the morale of Ney and his troops, he lied to the marshal about which forces were approaching on the right flank, telling him they were Grouchy's and not Blücher's. Ney sent horsemen out to spread the word to the troops: "*Vive l'Empereur! Soldats, voilà Grouchy!*" (Long live the Emperor! Soldiers, Grouchy is here!)

The French moved forward one last time, but facing heavy fire, their advance ground to a halt. Then Wellington arose and waved his hat three times as the signal for his forces to counterattack. Supplemented by the few light cavalry Wellington had left, forty thousand Allied soldiers fixed, or attached, bayonets and charged forward. Ney desperately ordered his men to hold their ground, but they could not. For the first time in their history, the Old Guard retreated, yelling "*La Garde Recule!*" (The Guard retreats!) as they did. As they withdrew, it became apparent to them that the forces on their right were not Grouchy's; they were on the verge of being caught in a huge trap. And increasing their fear was the thought that they had been the victims of betrayal, a fear that had been gnawing at them since Lieutenant General Bourmont had deserted.

At first Napoléon tried to halt the retreat, but it soon turned into a horrible rout. Without notifying Ney, the emperor boarded his dark blue and gold imperial coach and fled. The sight of that coach flying headlong away from the battle only increased the

The French retreat as they are pursued by English cavalry and infantry. Even Napoléon's Old Guard, vastly outnumbered, could not defeat the Allies.

panic felt by an already desperate French army. "All was lost by a moment of terrifying panic," said the official French army report. "Even the cavalry squadrons accompanying the Emperor were overthrown and disorganized by these tumultuous waves."

Wrote Thielmann's chief of staff, Carl von Clausewitz, later known as one of history's great military strategists, on Napoléon's decision to have the Old Guard attack frontally: "Never had Bonaparte committed a greater error. There has always been an immense difference between leading an invincible army in an orderly withdrawal in the face of an overwhelmingly superior force, and returning like a veritable fugitive, guilty of having lost and abandoned an entire army."

Aftermath

Actually, not all the French had panicked. The Young Guard, another division of the Imperial Guard, fought bravely against five-to-one odds and kept the village of Plancenoit out of Prussian hands until 9:00 P.M. Remnants of the Old Guard struggled to cover Napoléon's retreat. When the British asked General Pierre-Jacques Cambronne to surrender, he refused. Polite historians have recorded his words as "The Guard dies but never surrenders." Others have said he used far stronger language in replying to the British. Minutes later he took a bullet to the face, leaving him seriously wounded, but not dead.

Ney might have been able to turn the tide at Waterloo if Napoléon had given him reinforcements.

Ney, who had four horses shot out from under him during the day, was now on foot, brandishing a broken saber. His face was black from gunpowder, his uniform in tatters. Still he fought on, trying vainly to halt the retreat. "Come and see how a Marshal of France dies!" he yelled at his tattered troops as he led them into yet another charge.

Wellington in Battle

Where Napoléon had given over command of his forces to Marshal Ney, the duke of Wellington took personal control of his forces. His highly visible presence gave great comfort to his men and improved their morale. Starting at 6:00 A.M. on the day of the Battle of Waterloo, Wellington rode across the British lines on his chestnut horse, Copenhagen. His personal bravery was positively inspirational. At one point he galloped toward Hougoumont to rally a group of German Nassau troops who were threatening to desert. As he rode back, a few dissatisfied Nassauers fired at him. He never batted an eye but later remarked on how the fate of Europe might have been different if one of "those fellows" had had better aim.

Wrote one observer, quoted in John Naylor's *Waterloo*:

> He was everywhere. . . . The eye could turn in no direction that it did not perceive him either at hand or at a distance; galloping to charge the enemy or darting across the field to issue orders. Every [cannon] ball also . . . seemed fired, and every gun aimed at him. . . . But he suffered [allowed] nothing to check [stop] or engage him. . . . His entire concentrated attention, elusive aim, and intense thought were devoted impartially, imperturbably [calmly] and grandly to the Whole, and All.

Later in the day the duke made his headquarters below an elm tree at Mont-Saint-Jean just a quarter of a mile from the Allied outpost at la Haye Sainte. Later he went back to battle on horseback, going wherever he was needed to steady his troops' nerves. "Steadfast . . . ," he said at one point, "we must not be beat—what will they say in England." Wherever he went, his men cheered him, but Wellington would quiet them, saying: "No cheering, my lads, but forward and complete your victory!"

As the battle wound down, Wellington continued to risk his life in this manner. His troops protested, but the duke replied, "Never mind, let them fire away. The battle's won; my life is of no consequence now."

Wellington characteristically rides in the thick of his troops, in spite of the great personal danger to himself.

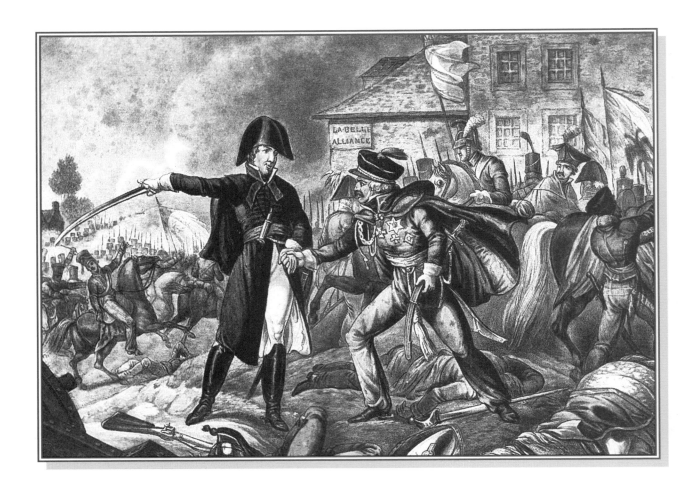

Blücher (right) meets Wellington on the battlefield of Waterloo. Ironically, the two had to speak to each other in the language of their enemy—French.

At one point he came upon Drouet. Thinking of how Louis XVIII would react to their disloyalty, he commented: "d'Erlon [Drouet], if we come out of this, you and I will be hanged."

Napoléon continued to flee south. He had hoped to meet a body of fresh troops but instead merely came upon rows of French dead. Said one French officer: "The dead in many places were piled two or three deep. The blood flowed from under them in streams. Through the principal street [of Ligny] the mud was red with blood, and the mud itself was composed of crushed bones and flesh."

At 9:30 P.M. Wellington and Blücher met. The aged Blücher was bent on revenge against Napoléon. Wrote Wellington, "Blücher wants to kill him, but I advised him to have nothing to do with so foul a transaction. . . . If the sovereigns wished to put him to death, they should appoint an executioner, which should not be me." The two Allied commanders also disagreed on what to call this momentous battle. Blücher wished to name it Belle-Alliance; Wellington preferred Waterloo. Ironically, the only way the two allies could understand each other was in the language of their vanquished enemy: French.

Artillery

The skilled use of artillery was key to the success of a Napoleonic-era army, and the weapons used had many forms.

The primary weapon used was the simple cannon, firing cannonballs in several sizes. For the French the most common sizes were four, eight, and twelve pounds; for the Prussians, six pounds and a few at twelve pounds; for the British, six and nine pounds. If fired into a mass of troops, a cannonball would go through them with frightening force, killing large numbers of men. Cannonballs could travel as far as four thousand yards but were most effective at ranges of half that distance.

Other variations of artillery also existed: canister, later named shrapnel for a British officer of the period who had invented it, grapeshot, incendiaries, howitzers, mortars, and rockets.

Canister consisted of a large number of iron balls—as many as a hundred—contained in a canister, much like in a shotgun shell and fired from a cannon. The canister would burst in midair, spraying these tiny balls in all directions.

A similar weapon was grapeshot, in which larger iron balls were loaded into the cannons without benefit of canisters. Grapeshot was effective only at very close range.

Incendiaries were either balls or casings filled with flammable materials and used against defenders of wooden structures or against such targets as ammunition storage dumps.

Rockets, howitzers, and mortars fired high trajectories and rained destruction straight down on their targets. Rockets were particularly favored by the British and could travel three thousand yards, but because of their inaccuracy, they were not particularly effective.

A French cannoneer leans with lit fuse at the ready.

Following this meeting, Wellington's forces, exhausted from a full day of horrific combat, gave up any pursuit of Napoléon's forces and turned the task over to Blücher. The iron-willed Prussian ordered his men to chase the French "so long as there is one man and one horse still standing."

At 10:00 P.M. Wellington wrote to his superior, Lord Bathurst, "My Lord, Napoléon has mustered, between the 10th and the 14th of this month, his 1st, 2nd, 3rd, 4th and 6th Army Corps, as well as the Imperial Guard and almost all of his cavalry on the Sambre [River]. . . . I have the pleasure of telling Your lordship that the army has never behaved better."

At 2:00 the next morning Blücher paused to write to an old friend: "The finest battle has been fought, the proudest victory won. . . ; we are now mopping up the stragglers. I had thought to shake up Napoléon's gang, but now it is almost over. I can write no more, for I am trembling all over; the effort has really been too great."

Then, despite his exhaustion, the seventy-two-year-old Blücher jumped back into the saddle to personally supervise the destruction of the rest of Napoléon's army.

CHAPTER SIX

Restoration, Saint Helena, and the Napoleonic Legend

The level of carnage at Waterloo was immense. In just one day and within a three-square-mile area, 47,000 men lay dead or wounded. One-half of all British infantry officers were casualties; one-third of the British cavalry was lost. Toward the battle's end Lord Uxbridge lost a leg to cannon fire. The cannonball that hit Uxbridge's knee had just missed Wellington's horse. "By God! I've lost my leg," cried Uxbridge. Wellington coolly responded, "Have you, by God?" Yet Wellington, who lost literally dozens of his most trusted officers—51 casualties on his general staff alone—could be moved by the slaughter. "Oh, do not congratulate me," a weeping Wellington told admirers back in Brussels, "I have lost all my friends."

The French lost 36 generals and 720 officers. Between 220 and 260 French guns were captured.

The overall casualty level at Waterloo on June 18 was equally disturbing:

Army	Number of Men	Killed or Wounded	Captured
Anglo-Dutch	67,000	17,415	N.A.
French	73,900	24,000	8,000
Prussian	48,000	6,998	N.A.

After the battle thousands of dead and wounded soldiers littered the battlefield. Local residents and undisciplined soldiers robbed the dead and dying of their valuables. So many men perished

A painting of the battlefield after Waterloo reveals the carnage that was left in its wake. At left, men are buried in mass graves while piles of dead—French, Prussian, and British alike, await burial.

that thousands were simply dumped into mass graves. As Wellington observed shortly after defeating Napoléon at Waterloo, "Nothing except a battle lost can be half so melancholy as a battle won."

Grouchy Redeems Himself

What had become of Grouchy? Late in the afternoon of June 18 his 25,000 troops finally caught up to Thielmann's 17,000 soldiers at Wavre and Limale, eventually defeating them in two essentially meaningless engagements. Although the Prussians had known of Napoléon's catastrophic defeat at Waterloo during the night of June 18-19, Grouchy did not learn of it until late in the morning of the nineteenth. A shocked Grouchy then ordered his forces to retreat through Namur and Givet. Where he had been excruciatingly slow and uncertain in pursuing the Prussians, in retreat he was masterful. At Philippeville on June 20, he met Marshal Soult who now commanded the 30,000-man remnant of the Armée du Nord that was abandoned by Napoléon. The combined 55,000-man force faced 66,000 of Blücher's troops and 52,000 of Wellington's. The French could have engaged in another battle, but morale was shattered. They retreated south for a few days, before Soult also abandoned his post, pleading ill health. Grouchy assumed command and continued his skillful withdrawal into France itself. His leadership was so brilliant that France's minister of war, Louis Davout, wrote to him, "You have rendered a service to France that will be held in repute [esteem] by the entire world."

"I Have Ended My Political Career"

Blücher steadily pursued the beaten French, looting towns as he went, for the Prussians were intent on avenging their defeats of 1806. When Blücher reached the French capital on July 4, he excitedly wrote to his wife: "Paris is mine!" So bitter was Blücher over past Prussian defeats that he had to be persuaded not to blow up a bridge, Pont de Jena, named after the famous Napoleonic triumph at Jena. Wellington also had to persuade Blücher from exacting harsh reprisals against the city.

Napoléon had reached Paris on Wednesday, June 21. Returning to the capital was critical for him, as the ranks of his domestic enemies were now growing rapidly. The pressure on him to abdicate once more was quickly building.

As Napoléon retreated, he concocted plans for staving off total defeat. He had written to his brother Joseph, who was his regent, that is, ruler in his absence, back in Paris:

> I believe the Deputies [legislators] will be made to understand that it is their duty to join me in saving France. . . . All is not lost by a long chalk. . . . I shall call up a *levée en masse* [mass recruitment] in Dauphine, at Lyons, in Burgundy, Lorraine and Champagne. . . . I shall soon have three hundred thousand soldiers under arms to face the enemy! . . . Then I'll simply crush them once and for all!

Napoléon and his aides leave the battlefield and abandon the Armée du Nord, which, without its leader, disintegrates in the background.

The Emperor Flees

In the disaster that followed the Old Guard's retreat, the Armée du Nord virtually fell apart. Napoléon barely kept ahead of the advancing Prussian calvarymen. At one point he abandoned his imperial coach—inside were gold, banknotes, and his sister's 300,000 franc diamond necklace—and hurriedly mounted a horse to avoid capture.

At Philippeville the emperor found many of his old commanders. Placing Soult in charge of what was left of his forces, he determined to call up reinforcements and fight again. But on reaching Laon in northern France, he abruptly changed his mind and headed for Paris. With his army defeated, Napoléon's political situation was also becoming precarious. He would, as he had in Egypt and Russia, abandon his vanquished army in order to reach the capital and consolidate what was left of his power.

But he had no guarantee of success, only the possibility of further violence, this time against his own people. He was ruthless enough to plan on such an eventuality. "If I return to Paris," Napoléon had informed General Henri Bertrand at Philippeville, "and I have to get my hands bloody, then I'll shove them in right up to the elbow!"

This was nonsense. On reaching Paris, Napoléon had demanded dictatorial powers. Instead, the following day the combined chambers of the French parliament demanded that he abdicate. He was furious but again abdicated in favor of his young son.

He spent the next week in a sort of suspended animation. Not only was he unsure of what to do, but Police Minister Joseph Fouché, who had assumed leadership of the provisional government, was unsure about what to do with him. Fouché barred French ships from carrying Napoléon without British permission, but he clearly wanted Napoléon away from Paris. Fouché feared that Napoléon still had enough popular and military support to attempt another seizure of power. On June 29 Napoléon, who realized such an attempt would ultimately be futile, left Malmaison on the outskirts of Paris, hoping eventually to reach the United States. He reached the port of Rochefort on the Bay of Biscay, and on July 8 set sail for America. He got only as far as Île d'Aix just a few miles offshore. Fearing that the treacherous Fouché would still be able to order his arrest by French naval authorities, Napoléon decided to entrust himself to the mercy of his British foes.

On Friday, July 14, he wrote to Great Britain's prince regent:

Royal Highness,

A prey [victim] to the factions which divide my country and to the hostility of the greatest powers of Europe, I have ended my political career, and I am going, like Themistocles, to seat myself at the hearth of the British people. I put myself under the protection of its laws, which I ask from Your Royal Highness, as from the most powerful, the most constant, and most generous of my enemies.

The next morning he boarded a nearby English warship, the 74-gun *Bellerophon*, and surrendered to its captain. He now had hopes that he would be allowed to live in Great Britain. Despite the decades of war between Napoléon and the British, he admired and respected them as a people. Before his first abdication he had written to one of his ministers to inquire if Great Britain would grant him asylum.

Although some in Great Britain wished to grant him asylum, exile there was not to be. Fearing another Napoleonic return, the British government instead decided that Napoléon should travel to where he would never disturb the peace of Europe again.

"To Die Is Nothing"

Napoléon's destination was Saint Helena, a tiny, British island in the middle of the south Atlantic Ocean, 1,920 kilometers west of the African nation of Angola. He would stage no escape from this island. Here he was no longer an emperor; he was a prisoner.

At first Napoléon lived in a little building in the garden of an English family, the Balcombes, and became especially close to thirteen-year-old Betsy Balcombe. The two played cards and blind man's bluff; at both games he cheated.

Later he was provided with a house on Deadwood Plain. Napoléon hated Saint Helena's miserable, damp weather. He hated the island's many rats—one of which even jumped out of his hat. He hated the regulations that forced him to travel about the island only in the company of a British soldier, and because of that he rarely went outside his house.

But above all he hated the island's British governor, Sir Hudson Lowe. Of him, Napoléon wrote, "I have seen Prussians, Tartars, Cossacks, Kalmucks [Mongolians] and many others, but never before in my life have I seen so ill-favored and forbidding a countenance."

Napoléon pursued a life of sad idleness on Saint Helena, staring for hours at clouds or flowers, or just sitting in his bath. Some said his hand had worn a smooth spot in his soap dish. He complained to Sir Hudson Lowe: "The island is too small for me. The climate is not like ours, it is not our sun, nor does it have

A brooding Napoléon on board the British warship Bellerophon *after surrendering to the captain.*

"St. Helena, a Small Island"

The south Atlantic island of Saint Helena that served as Napoléon's home for the last six years of his life was one of the most isolated places on earth. It is a small volcanic island, just ten miles long and six miles wide, very mountainous and heavily forested.

Before its discovery by the Portuguese on May 21, 1502, Saint Helen's Day, the island was uninhabited. Saint Helena's first European inhabitants were goats that were set free by its discoverer, Admiral Joao da Nova, and soon numbered in the thousands. Its first human inhabitant was a Portuguese nobleman who exiled himself as penance for renouncing his Catholic faith in favor of Islam.

In 1659 the British East India Company established the first permanent settlement.

As remote a piece of real estate as Saint Helena was, Napoléon had long known of its existence. While in school studying British possessions, he had scribbled in his notebook: "St. Helena, a small island." He had even considered capturing it and using it as a military base. In 1804 he thought that "1,200 to 1,500 men will be required [to take the island]. . . . The English are in no way expecting this expedition and it will be a simple matter to surprise them."

To this day Saint Helena remains a British possession.

Napoléon, on the island of Saint Helena, surveys his new "kingdom." At right is the house in which Napoléon lived.

our seasons. Everything breathes a mortal boredom here. The situation is disagreeable, unhealthy. There is no water. This part of the island is a desert. It has chased all its inhabitants away."

He longed for the pomp and glory he no longer had. Often he would awake and sadly state, "I dreamt of Paris."

Suffering from stomach cancer, Napoléon's life was slowly slipping away. On coming out of his bath on October 10, 1820, Napoléon fainted. For months he remained bedridden and mainly listless. In April 1821 he composed his will: "I wish my ashes to rest on the banks of the Seine, in the midst of that French people which I have loved so much. . . . I die before my time, killed by the English [government] and its hired assassins."

He died in the early evening of May 5, 1821. His passing must have been a release, for the burden of what once had been was a great weight on his spirit. "To die is nothing," he once stated, "but to live defeated is to die every day."

A statue entitled "The Last Days of Napoléon" depicts the former emperor as ill and near the end of his life, but still dreaming of victory, battle plan in his lap.

Why Napoléon Lost

Since 1815 historians have pondered over the lessons of Waterloo. The Armée du Nord was composed of hardened veterans and soldier for soldier was a better fighting force than either Wellington's or Blücher's armies. Yet in a tremendous irony Napoléon, one of the premier military strategists of all time, and even after deciding on a basically sound plan, committed error after error and doomed his army to overwhelming defeat.

Napoléon had selected an ill-equipped group of generals to lead his army. Partially he had little choice. Berthier was dead; Mortier was ill; André Masséna, whom both Napoléon and Wellington rated as brilliant, showed no interest in joining this latest adventure; Baron Jomini was with the Allies. Bourmont defected at the last minute. But Napoléon had other able strategists whom he refused to use such as Joachim Murat, perhaps the ablest cavalry leader in Europe. Capable subordinates such as Louis Davout, the duke of Auerstedt, left behind in Paris, or Louis-Gabriel Suchet, leading an army on the Upper Rhine, were given other commands. Some said that Napoléon surrounded himself with lesser generals on purpose. "To secure his grasp over his people and to cow the opposition of the other crowned

The Execution of Marshal Ney

After being arrested in August and convicted of treason, Marshal Michel Ney returned to the room in the Luxembourg Palace in Paris where he was kept prisoner. At 4:00 on the morning of December 7, 1815, he was awakened. His jailers had brought his wife, his sister, and his two sons to him. When Ney told his family that he would be executed that very morning, his wife fainted. His sons stood silent, bewildered by what they were hearing.

Once she had revived, Ney's wife hurried to the Louvre Palace to beg Louis XVIII for her husband's life. She was curtly informed that His Majesty could not be disturbed; he was having breakfast.

Ney was led out onto a Paris street and stood before a firing squad of twelve soldiers. He stubbornly refused to kneel and be blindfolded, as was customary. "A man such as I does not get down on his knees," he stormed. Then he placed his hand in front of his heart and demanded, "Soldiers, straight at the heart."

Passersby stopped to stare at the unannounced execution. The drums began to beat faster and faster. The firing squad cried out: "Long live the king" and fired their muskets.

Despite Ney's instructions, three of the shots had hit him in the face. Marshal Michel Ney, the bravest of the brave, was dead.

Or was he? As the years passed, legends grew that Ney had merely feigned death. Some claimed he became a schoolmaster in Third Creek, North Carolina. Others say he was seen visiting a former comrade in Indiana.

heads of Europe he knew he needed a tremendous demonstration of personal success . . . ," wrote historian David Chandler in *Waterloo: The Hundred Days*. "In 1815 it had to be the Emperor's very own unquestioned success."

Yet, Napoléon soon made his task all the more difficult by placing his remaining generals in roles they were unsuited for: Soult as chief of staff; Ney on his left wing; Grouchy on his right. He procrastinated and gave unclear orders to his subordinates. Then at Waterloo Napoléon entrusted the unreliable Ney with overall command of the attack on Wellington. The result was a disaster.

Napoléon also seemed sluggish at Waterloo. He failed to follow up on opportunities, and when he exerted himself, it was to parade before his troops and receive their cheers rather than to carefully plot strategy or coordinate his numerically inferior forces. His behavior contrasted not only with his former brilliance, but also with the steady performance of his adversaries, Wellington and Blücher.

Napoléon's troops were uncommonly brave at Waterloo. So were Wellington's. Blücher's forces were tenacious and untiring. The difference in determining the outcome was the quality of French generalship. To call it incompetent might be generous; its errors were legion. Napoléon himself had delayed in attacking Blücher at Ligny, failed to use Lobau in crushing Blücher, neglected to immediately pursue the defeated Blücher, been slow to attack Wellington on June 18, and failed to assign Ney the Imperial Guard as reinforcements when they could have made a major difference. Soult had been a disaster as chief of staff, neglecting to coordinate the border crossing and, along with Napoléon, failing to promptly and coherently send out orders to subordinates. Vandamme had needlessly delayed at Gilly; Drouet had wasted a day marching pointlessly between Quatre Bras and Ligny; while Grouchy's tortoiselike pursuit of the Prussians was a key to the French defeat.

Ney had committed numerous errors. His sluggishness in attacking at Quatre Bras allowed Wellington to plan his brilliant defense of Waterloo. At Waterloo itself Ney exhibited extreme slowness in using artillery against Hougoumont. He critically failed to support his infantry with cavalry then failed to support his cavalry with infantry. He mistakenly used a division-width formation in his attack, and along with Drouet had neglected to spike the British guns they had overrun.

Napoléon, Ney, Grouchy, and Drouet all committed serious mistakes during this brief but disastrous adventure. But as plodding as Ney and Grouchy were as the Battle of Waterloo began, by personal bravery and skillful withdrawal they redeemed themselves as the campaign crashed to an end.

The great Napoléon, however, once more abandoned his army and fled for his life.

Napoléon at Waterloo. His defeat would forever end French aspirations of European takeover and would change the map of Europe.

The Map of Europe

With Napoléon defeated, the Congress of Vienna reconvened and completed its work. France's borders were reduced to those of 1789, and it was made to pay a compensation of 700,000 francs to the victorious Allies. Although few French and fewer Allies wished to restore Louis XVIII to the throne, the British did, and they had their way. Until his death in 1824 Louis XVIII reigned as king of France and did something Napoléon could not: subdue Spain. After Spaniards overthrew King Ferdinand VII in 1821, Louis's armies marched into Madrid and easily restored him to the throne in 1823.

The Congress of Vienna drew up a map of Europe based on old dynasties rather than new nationalist feelings. Germany, composed of a large number of independent states of which Austria and Prussia were the largest, and Italy, divided into such areas as the Papal States, the kingdom of Sardinia and the kingdom of the Two Sicilies, remained disunited. Belgium was given to the Netherlands; Norway, to Sweden; Finland, to Russia. Poland remained divided among Prussia, Russia, and Austria. Austria ruled over numerous nationalities beside the Poles—Hungarians, Czechs, Slovaks, Italians, Croats, and Slovenes. Russia similarly ruled over such groups as the Ukrainians, Lithuanians, Latvians, and Estonians.

With nationalism growing, such a situation could not last for long. In 1830 Belgians freed themselves from the Dutch. In 1848 and 1849 unrest spread throughout Europe. The Croats rebelled against the Hungarians; the Hungarians, Italians, and Czechs against the Austrians. Disturbances arose in Berlin and Vienna. Short-lived republics were proclaimed in Venice and Rome.

Although the Hungarians won permanent concessions from the Austrians, most of the advances of 1848 were soon overthrown by the established monarchies. Yet nationalism could not be held back for long. The movement was not only political but artistic. In literature, poetry, philosophy, and music, nationalism became a powerful force. By 1870 the Italians united under the leadership of the kingdom of Savoy. They were soon followed by the Germans, who in 1871 formed an empire of their own under Prussian leadership.

The fires of nationalism would eventually fuel European hatreds and rivalries that would erupt into World War I in 1914. Despite the millions of deaths that conflict caused, the vicious strains of nationalism found in Germany's National Socialism and Italy's Fascism would plunge the continent into horrific warfare once more in 1939.

"An Empire Is Lightning"

Despite the disasters that had twice forced Napoléon to abdicate and that had cost France hundreds of thousands of casualties, Napoléon retained a sizable core of admirers in France. Even when Blücher was closing in on Paris, Napoléon's supporters among the working classes unrealistically plotted a coup to keep him in power.

With Napoléon at Saint Helena, his legend grew. He had, after all, been the towering figure of his age, a great military and civil figure. Those who romantically glorified war and conquest turned him into their hero. Those who chafed under Bourbon and then Orléans rule thought that a return to Napoleonic-style rule would bring badly needed reform to France. Legends grew about Napoléon's death; some thought he was poisoned with arsenic. Even the royalist writer and politician François Chateaubriand, no admirer of Napoléon, was forced to admit: "This bloodstained soldier adorned his throne with the trophies of art, and made Paris the seat of taste as well as power. . . . The weight of the chains he imposed on France was forgotten in their splendor; it was glorious to follow him, even as a conscript [draftee]."

In France the Bourbons remained unpopular. In 1830 Louis XVIII's brother, Charles X, was overthrown, and the Chamber of Deputies elected the duke of Orleans, Louis-Philippe, as their king. The authoritarian Louis-Philippe did not learn from his predecessors

What Happened to Waterloo's Key Players?

Besides Napoléon and Ney, what happened to Waterloo's key players? Marshal Nicholas Soult, Napoléon's chief of staff, went into exile but returned to France in 1819. Under King Louis-Philippe he became prime minister and in 1847 was designated marshal general of France, only the fourth person so named.

Marshal Emmanuel de Grouchy, commander of Napoléon's right wing, was charged with treason but, because of his mental state, was found incompetent to stand trial. He went into exile in America but returned to France in 1819. He was reinstated as a marshal in 1831.

General Pierre Cambronne, the Old Guard officer who boldly refused to surrender to the British, was nonetheless taken prisoner by them. He recovered from his wounds and on his return to France was sentenced to death for treason but was pardoned by Louis XVIII.

Prince Jérôme Bonaparte, Napoléon's brother and the commander of the Sixth Division, fled to Germany and later to Italy and Switzerland. When Napoléon III restored the empire, Jérôme became a marshal of France in 1850 and president of the senate in 1852. He died in 1860.

Joachim Murat, whom Napoléon stubbornly refused to use at Waterloo, returned to Italy, where he was captured by local police and immediately executed by a firing squad in 1815.

Lieutenant General Étienne-Maurice Gérard, commander of Napoléon's Fourth Corps, was pensioned off from the army but later returned to active service and was promoted to marshal in 1830.

The prince of Orange, commander of Wellington's First Corps at Quatre Bras and Waterloo, recovered from wounds suffered at Waterloo and became known in his own country, if nowhere else, as the Hero of Waterloo. In 1840 his father abdicated, and the prince succeeded him as King William II of the Netherlands. He died in March 1849.

The aged Prussian hero of Waterloo, Gebhard von Blücher, was in poor health when he left Paris for home in October 1815. Not only was he physically ill, but he was suffering from delusions. At home in Breslau his problems only increased as he became increasingly mentally ill. However, he still had enough energy left to attend to agriculture on his estate and to occasionally wager far more than he could afford. Blücher died in September 1819.

After Waterloo the duke of Wellington wrote that he wished he had fought his last battle. He had in a military sense, but he fought a variety of governmental and political battles in the decades that followed. A firm believer in preserving aristocratic interests, Wellington later served as prime minister of Great Britain, and often espoused unpopular positions. It was when he placed iron shutters on his London home to protect it from mobs that he earned the nickname the Iron Duke. He died in 1852 at the age of eighty-three.

The execution of Joachim Murat, who reportedly uncovered his chest and gave the word, "fire."

Napoléon III, like his uncle, had aspirations of glory. He became dictator of France and also proclaimed himself emperor. He, too, would be defeated.

and was overthrown in the disturbances that rocked the European continent in 1848.

Napoléon's popularity was still so powerful that in 1841 Louis-Philippe ordered his remains brought back to Paris and buried with honors in a monumental tomb at the church of Les Invalides. To win popular favor, Louis-Philippe even shouted "*Vive l'empereur!*" (Long live the emperor!) during the ceremony.

The hopes of Bonapartists for a restoration of the imperial line rested in Napoléon's son, Napoléon II, also known as the duke of Reichstadt and the king of Rome. But after 1815 the child was a virtual prisoner of his Austrian relatives. In 1830 his uncle, Joseph Bonaparte, argued that Napoléon II should replace Charles X, but the would-be emperor died of tuberculosis in 1832 without ever occupying the throne of France.

The Napoleonic mantle thus fell to Louis Napoléon, the son of Louis Bonaparte. Twice—in 1836 and 1840—Louis Napoléon unsuccessfully attempted to seize power in France. His chance finally came in 1848, when he became president of the republic, which had replaced Louis-Philippe and the monarchy. In December 1851 he became dictator of France and the following year proclaimed himself Emperor Napoléon III. Somewhat less warlike than his uncle, Napoléon III nonetheless involved France from 1854 to 1856 in the Crimean War against Russia; against Austria in Italy in 1859; and in establishing a French puppet empire in Mexico in 1864. But he saw his empire come crashing down at the hands of the Prussians. Humiliatingly defeated in the Franco-Prussian War, Napoléon III's Second Empire collapsed in September 1870. Yet the cult of Napoléon did not die. Bonapartists remained a force in French political life for decades. Authors have written over 180,000 books on Napoléon's life. When Hitler conquered France in 1940, he made a trip to Paris to visit Napoléon's tomb. He also arranged for Napoléon II's reburial at les Invalides. The anthem of Corsica, the "Ajacienne," is a hymn of praise to Napoléon I, who was born there. In 1971 on the 150th anniversary of Napoléon's death, France outdid itself in commemorating him and the glories of his ill-fated empire. "A nation is a tree," remarked the former French minister of cultural affairs André Malraux, "but an empire is lightning."

Glossary

abdicate: To resign as a monarch.

armada: A large naval fleet.

Bourbon: Royal house of France; swept away by the French Revolution but temporarily restored after Napoléon's fall.

concordat: A formal agreement between the Roman Catholic Church and a sovereign state, usually regulating church-state relations.

conscription: Forced military service.

coup d'état: A forcible seizure of a government.

cuirassiers: Cavalrymen named for the breast-plates, or cuirasses, that they wore in action.

émigrés: Royalist nobility and clergy who fled France after the revolution of 1789.

Enlightenment: The eighteenth-century movement based on science and nonreligious beliefs that rational, humanistic ideals could benefit humankind in all aspects of its existence.

feculia: A small sailing vessel.

guerrilla warfare: Warfare based on small, mobile, irregular forces, often out of uniform, which employs surprise attacks, sabotage, and attacks on supply lines and depots.

guillotine: A device used for execution by beheading during the French Revolution.

Hanover: An independent state in north-central Germany. In 1714 the elector (ruler) of Hanover became George I of England. Hanover was annexed by Prussia in 1866.

hors de combat: Disabled.

monarchists: Believers in the system of monarchy.

Nassau: An independent German duchy; annexed by Prussia in 1866.

nationalism: A belief that individuals owe their greatest loyalty to their nation-state; has often enabled peoples to free themselves from foreign oppression but has also led to aggression and hostility toward other nationalities.

plebiscite: A general vote of the people to approve or disapprove of a major government policy or choice of ruler.

referendum: A vote by citizens on a specific issue of public policy.

regent: One who rules while a king is incapacitated or underage.

royalists: Believers in the system of monarchy.

sappers: Military trench diggers.

scorched-earth policy: Destruction of everything of value, particularly so that it may not fall into the hands of an enemy.

sepoy: A native soldier serving under the British colonial rule of the Indian subcontinent.

tricolor: The blue, white, and red flag of the French Republic and the Napoleonic empire.

vassal state: A supposedly independent state which in actuality is under the control of another.

For Further Reading

Trevor N. Dupuy, *The Battle of Austerlitz: Napoleon's Greatest Victory*. New York: Macmillan, 1968. While Napoléon was far from a brilliant strategist at Waterloo, this book offers a good look at him at the peak of his power. Well-illustrated and featuring a helpful chronology.

Manuel Komroff, *The Battle of Waterloo: One Hundred Days of Destiny*. New York: Macmillan, 1964. Similar to Dupuy's *The Battle of Austerlitz* in format and in illustrations and chronology.

Patrick Pringle, *Napoleon's Hundred Days*. London and New York: Frederick Warner, 1968. Similar in subject matter to Komroff's book, minus chronology, but at a slightly lower reading level.

Frances Winwar, *Napoleon and the Battle of Waterloo*. New York: Random House, 1953. Contains far more on Napoléon's early career and far less on Waterloo than the title would suggest.

Works Consulted

Julia Blackburn, *The Emperor's Last Stand: A Journey to St. Helena.* New York: Pantheon, 1992. An intriguing blend of history and travelogue on Napoléon and the island of Saint Helena.

Duc de Castries, *The Lives of the Kings and Queens of France.* New York: Alfred A. Knopf, 1979. A finely illustrated and highly sympathetic look at France's Bourbon monarchs.

Lord Chalfont, ed., *Waterloo.* New York: Alfred A. Knopf, 1980. A unique study of the battle, featuring the viewpoints of three expert British, French, and German military historians. The French historian's viewpoint is surprisingly sympathetic to Napoléon's actions at Waterloo.

David Chandler, *Waterloo: The Hundred Days.* New York: Macmillan, 1980. A coherent and well-illustrated study by a British expert on the Napoleonic period. Contains a section on touring the battlefield.

Charles Fenyvesi, *Splendor in Exile: The Ex-Majesties of Europe.* Washington: New Republic Books, 1979. A fascinating look at the exiled former monarchs and the pretenders to the thrones of Europe. Contains a chapter on the house of Bonaparte.

Henry Lachouque, *The Last Days of Napoléon's Empire.* Translated by Lovett F. Andrews. New York: Orion Press, 1967. A detailed look at Napoléon immediately after Waterloo. Also features a section on Waterloo itself. Particularly illuminating is the text of an anonymous French officer who was at Waterloo detailing Napoléon's mistakes.

————, *Waterloo.* London: Arms and Armour Press, 1978. A beautifully illustrated book, supplemented with a helpful listing of units in the battle, but marred by an often unclear text.

Elizabeth Longford, *Wellington: The Years of the Sword.* New York: Harper and Row, 1969. A standard biography of Wellington. Contains a lengthy section on Waterloo.

Claude Manceron, *Napoleon Recaptures Paris: March 20, 1815.* Translated by George Unwin. New York: W. W. Norton, 1968. A highly detailed recounting of Napoléon's return to power.

John Naylor, *Waterloo.* New York: Macmillan, 1960. A good, straightforward history of the battle, told in no-nonsense but highly understandable fashion.

Alan Schom, *One Hundred Days: Napoleon's Road to Waterloo.* New York: Atheneum, 1992. A well-written and informative popular history of Napoléon's great adventure. Highly recommended.

John Sutherland, *Men of Waterloo.* Englewood Cliffs, NJ: Prentice-Hall, 1967. A work that features a greater than usual amount of information on military practices and conditions of the time. It also focuses to a greater extent than normal on the ordinary soldiers of the day.

Index

Picture Credits

About the Author

David Pietrusza has written for numerous publications, including *Modern Age*, *The Journal of Social and Political Studies*, *Academic Reviewer*, and *The New Oxford Review*. For two years he produced the nationally syndicated radio program, *National Perspectives*. He is also the author of *The End of the Cold War*, *The Invasion of Normandy*, *The Mysterious Death of John F. Kennedy*, and the *Cultural Revolution*, all published by Lucent.

Mr. Pietrusza has also written extensively on the subject of baseball. He is the president of the Society for American Baseball Research and managing editor of *Total Baseball*, the official encyclopedia of Major League Baseball. His three books on baseball are *Minor Miracles: The Legends and Lure of Minor League Baseball*, *Major Leagues,* and *Baseball's Canadian-American League*. In 1994 Pietrusza served as a consultant for PBS's Learning Link on-line system and produced the documentary "Local Heroes" for PBS affiliate WMHT.

He lives with his wife, Patricia, in Scotia, New York.